SMITHING
with the
HANDHELD PNEUMATIC HAMMER

SMITHING

with the

HANDHELD PNEUMATIC HAMMER

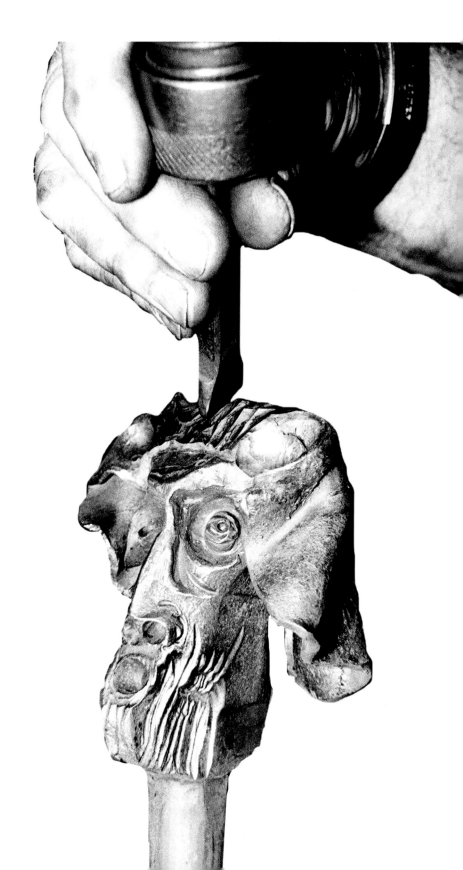

E. A. CHASE

Notice to Reader

The information and material in this book, to the best of our knowledge, were accurate and true at the time of writing. All recommendations are made without guarantee on the part of the author or the publisher. The author and publisher disclaim any liability in connection with the use of information contained in this book or the application of such information.

The reader is expressly warned to consider and adopt all safety precautions regarding working with a pneumatic hammer and blacksmithing. Furthermore, the reader is warned to avoid all potential hazards. By following the instructions herein, the reader willingly assumes all risks in connection with such instructions.

Hardcover ISBN: 978-1-879535-30-5

Production Notes

Unless otherwise stated all photos were taken and all drawings and images were done by and are copyright © E.A. Chase.

Cover and Layout Design: Sonya Boushek
Indexed: Dianna Haught, Words by Haught
Publisher: Alan E. Krysan

 SkipJack Press

An Imprint of Finney Company
5995 149th Street West, Suite 105,
Apple Valley, MN 55124
www.finneyco.com

Printed in United States of America

This book is dedicated to my wife Joy who is the source of much of the substance in my life and work.

CONTENTS

1 PNEUMATIC TOOL SELECTION

Page 1

2 THE DESIGN AND FORGING OF TOOL BITS FOR PNEUMATIC HAMMERS

Page 7

3 BASIC SUPPORT EQUIPMENT

Page 23

4 INCISING AND GOUGING FOR HOT HEAVY METALS; COLD MARKING FOR HOT WORK

Page 33

PREFACE

In 1995 while recovering from hip replacement surgery I decided to start gathering the photographs, sketches and notes that I had accumulated on the use of the handheld pneumatic hammer. I wanted to explore the feasibility of writing a book on the subject. By this time the pneumatic hammer had already been a major asset in my forge for twenty years. I started to use this tool for cold marking and center punching applications prior to hot working. The clearly identifiable and accurate marking was an improvement over hand marking to such a degree that I adopted the method immediately.

I knew that a book on this subject could be a very useful addition to the smithing library. I could not find any contemporary publications on handheld pneumatic hammers directed at the artist metalsmith or, for that matter, anyone else. I assumed that a book on the subject would need many illustrations to support the text and that I would need to have commissions that required lots of pneumatic hammer work. It looked like a long term task. I did not realize at the time what a serious commitment it would take from me and ultimately from my wife to complete the task.

In the meantime at California Blacksmith Association (CBA) and Artist-Blacksmith's Association of America (ABANA) conferences I had many opportunities to demonstrate the methods I had been developing. The interest generated at these demonstrations encouraged me to continue the project. I retired in 2010 and have devoted my energies to finishing this work.

I have completed this book with some conscious oversights. I know there are other smiths working with the pneumatic hammer at various skill levels. But because of my lack of mobility and age I could not uncover them to make this book act as a wider vehicle for the work being accomplished with these exciting tools. However I would like to recommend becoming familiar with the work of Corky Storer of Washington State, whose sculpture with the pneumatic hammer is inspiring, and with Peter Fels of California whose whimsey and humor is deftly rendered with the pneumatic hammer.

When this book was in its early stages I gave it to a friend to critique. Ali Americupan knew my work very well, having helped me install many of my pieces; I depended on his rational approach to problem solving. As a college teacher of metal arts, Ali was tuned into teaching. His critique of my early draft set the structural foundation for the book.

Mike Tuciarone took the manuscript from its primitive state of near predigital evolution and transformed it into a formatted, disciplined, and useful (I hope) and readable manuscript. He has given new meaning to friendship by his commitment to this project in spite of an already formidable workload as an Apple software engineer.

I needed to run the manuscript by some exceptional smiths who are familiar with my work, the techniques I use, and the larger picture of how this all fits in to contemporary metalsmithing.

Peter Fels, who lives and works on a bluff high above the Pacific in Big Sur with his wife Phoebe, is in a perpetual process of building an architectural fantasy that they call home. When Peter is working on other than his home, the work is often with a pneumatic hammer. Thus the reason I court his opinion on this book. His years of artistic metalsmithing experience include some beautiful and wildly eccentric musical instruments, lots of nonferrous domestic hardware, and "wearable" art; all very unique interpretations in a Post Art Nouveau genre.

Michael Bondi has been a working in metals since the early 70's in his forge in Berkeley and later in Richmond, California. Michael has an excellent working knowledge of a wide range of techniques, architectural periods, and a well rounded understanding of forgeable alloys. His successful career has been recognized with the Alex Bealer Award for his contributions to the art of blacksmithing.

Michael reached way beyond his role in reviewing this book to take on the task of improving photos that had been damaged by a corruption of my files and to recruit a graphics designer, Lauren Donohue, to help jump start the stalled process to finish this book. Finally, Michael promoted the book to the publisher of SkipJack Press with such conviction that I was welcomed to submit the book for publication. His commitment to this book was vital to its publication, and I am grateful for his friendship.

My wife Joy's editing skill were honed by her lifelong love of the written word. Her impressive command of the grammarian's craft combined with a career as an Environmental Analyst with its subsequent precise language requirements gave her the authority an editor needs and were crucial to making this a readable work.

I gratefully acknowledge my publisher Alan Krysan of Skipjack Press for taking the book over its final hurdle and to the presses with his professional guidance, encouragement and great enthusiasm. Graphic designer, Sonya Boushek, shaped the manuscript and created a visually artful design that is engaging and enhances the books useability.

Finally, my heartfelt thanks to the many blacksmiths and metalsmiths who encouraged me to get this book finished. Without your nagging, it might have slipped into the realm of the undone.

INTRODUCTION

This book is meant for the metalsmith who has already achieved some working knowledge of metal forming techniques using traditional hand hammer methods. As such, I do not intend to encourage the displacement of the hand hammer from its traditional role but rather to help enlarge the technical vocabulary of the artist/smith. New techniques inevitably produce not only different results; their influence will also be apparent in how the work is conceived and rendered. The process in getting to your envisioned form can be quite different from the traditional hand process. The pneumatic hammer does not mimic the hand hammer; it has its own "personality," and makes its own accommodations and demands on the smith.

As used in this book references to "pneumatic hammer" are to the handheld pneumatic hammer. The pneumatic driven power hammer is a different beast.

I first began using the pneumatic hammer on an incidental basis during the '70s for the conventional tasks of riveting and light cutting operations on my metalwork. As I became more familiar with the characteristics of the tool I started to realize that its unique features could be advantageous in other applications, particularly to reduce the tedium of tasks requiring repetitive blows such as texturing and peening. Another characteristic soon caught my attention: velocity. The speed of the bit striking the work is so rapid that deformation is significantly more localized than comparable blows with a hand hammer. This characteristic can provide, as I hope to show later, some interesting techniques. In addition to blows per minute (BPM) and velocity, control is a major asset of the air hammer; very precise work is possible with a good, controllable tool.

With a range of 900 to 2500 blows per minute (BPM) for the hammers covered in this book compared with what is possible by hand, you can correctly assume that it should be possible to move more metal with pneumatics than by hand. An individual blow with a hand hammer (factoring in the weight of the hammer) can provide much more energy per blow than all but perhaps the largest of handheld pneumatic hammers. This distinction is more than compensated for by the BPM and velocity of the latter. This basic difference provides the reason for the variations in process and end product between the two methods...and also my justification for writing this hopefully instructional book.

During a normal day at my forge my .401 and .498 hammers are kept plugged into my air supply and ready for use. On "hot iron" days they will be used for cold center punching and line tracing for layout, hot carving and incising, slitting, cutting, peening and riveting. On "cold working" days they are used almost exclusive of the hand hammer for forming everything from floral details to large-scale objects in non-ferrous sheet. They have become the dominant and most used hand tools in my shop.

The heavier and more powerful .680 shank hammer is used almost entirely for hot work such as punching, drifting, cutting and upsetting where the stationary power hammer is inappropriate or where a hand hammer would be the less efficient choice. All of these air tools are supported by an array of specially forged hammer bits that have evolved on an "as needed" basis.

If this subject arouses your curiosity, hear what I have to say and see what I have to show you, but remember to listen to yourself as the ultimate guide to your working methodology and vision. What I present in this book is based on personal work practices that have, as yet, not been subject to the refinement of tradition. Perhaps you can add to this approach with the knowledge gained from your own practice!

A SERENDIPITOUS TALE

Way back when I first considered the pneumatic hammer for inclusion in my blacksmith tool inventory, I thought of it only in the context of how it might be useful for the more mundane riveting chores I occasionally encountered; after all, I reasoned, it is a "riveting gun." Having experienced the process for a short time while working in the aircraft industry, I knew its advantages, and I thought I understood its limitations as well. It registered casually on my wish list.

I eventually found a used 4X.401 pneumatic hammer at a surplus store for an unbelievable twenty-five cents. The bargain price was irresistible for what appeared to be an industrial level tool, even in the 1969 economy. Upon returning to my shop with the prize I adapted it to my compressor and soon realized the tool was frozen for lack of lubrication! Not easily discouraged, I dismantled the hammer, lubricated and cleaned it, and finding that the seizing caused no lasting damage to the bore or piston, I connected it to my compressor, and it was reborn, no, resurrected. This hammer gradually became, (over a period of the next twenty-some years), the tooling and development source for much of the .401 hammer material in this book. Without fanfare, the hammer finally wheezed its last gasp about ten years ago and was retired to be replaced by an almost identical new tool (some things hardly change). Do I enjoy this little tale of metamorphosis, serendipity, frugality, and, oh yes, lubrication? You bet I do, it's a blacksmith's kind of story.

CAUTION

The pneumatic hammer can potentially cause shock and vibration damage to nerve and tissue of the hands, arms and ears. Medical studies have linked repetitive motion, and particularly high vibration (like pneumatic hammers), to nerve damage such as carpal tunnel syndrome.

The pneumatic hammer is capable of launching tool bits at deadly velocity if the trigger is activated when the tool bit is unrestrained - with possible catastrophic consequences.

These injuries, however, can be avoided or reduced for craftpersons using available safety devices and good (listen to your body) common sense work habits. For those of us who will turn a deaf ear to our bodies if the excitement is running common sense off the track, or if a schedule is looming threateningly in your guilt-ridden mind, hear this TAKE REASONABLE PRECAUTIONS. Use vibration absorbing gloves whenever possible, and talk to your doctor about hand exercises to relieve the strain of your work. Wear hearing and eye protection, safety shoes, and filter masks when appropriate. Always use a retainer on your handheld pneumatic hammer.

Take the time to protect your body, serve as a good model to others, and enjoy a long and healthy life.

CHAPTER 1

PNEUMATIC
~~~~~ Tool ~~~~~
SELECTION

GENERAL CHARACTERISTICS

I will not suggest brand names for you to buy, instead I will approach the subject of tool selection based on performance characteristics that are vital to the smith's application. Blows per minute (BPM) is an important parameter but must be considered in its relation to the length of the tool's stroke and diameter of the bore. In pneumatic hammer design, the longer the stroke the greater the impact potential per blow (at a given bore diameter). The ratio of BPM to stroke is determined by how long it takes for a complete stroke cycle; therefore the longer the stroke the lower the BPM. The trade off of more impact for less BPM for most metalwork applications creates a good balance of working criteria (except for some light peening applications tasks which would benefit from rapid, low impact surfacing to save time on these dreary tasks.) See Figure 1.6.

Cylinder bore diameter usually increases in proportion to the tool bit shank diameter. Along with stroke, cylinder bore and BPM, control is a vital component of air tool performance. Control of the tool's ability to deliver blows is perhaps the most important factor of all. Determined by the throttling sensitivity of the trigger design, control should allow for the softest tap to full power with absolute predictability. Control, control, control cannot be overemphasized.

In order to simplify the classification of pneumatic hammers, in this book I will use the shank diameter of the tool bits appropriate to the hammer to designate its size. For example, a .401 shank tool bit fits a .401 hammer.

Tools designed for industrial use all have alloy steel barrels. The smaller capacity tools will be constructed with an aluminum alloy pistol-grip handle (at about a right angle to barrel, at the rear of the tool) or sometimes with offset handles (located about two-thirds of the way up the tool barrel). I personally prefer the pistol grip configuration for both the .401 and the .498 hammers, which I feel offers more control, less wrist strain and a more comfortable distance from hotwork for the trigger hand. The larger tools (.680 diameter and larger) will have forged steel "C" shaped handles which will put your trigger hand in direct line with the barrel. Do not squander money, time, material and your good name by trying to substitute cheap tools designed for the consumer market. The performance the smith needs is only found in hammers rated "industrial." Many industrial pneumatic tool suppliers carry Asian made copies of American made industrial tools that have the same physical specifications and are superficially identical to their American counterparts. I cannot personally vouch for the copycat hammers, having not tried any of them beyond an initial performance review where I found that they often lack the trigger sensitivity (control) that I expect of original American made tools. Since my testing lacked a control and was riddled with subjective criteria, all I can really offer with this comparison is caution. Some suppliers have maintained that some of the imports they sell are commonly substituted for the more costly domestic products by industrial users. The copycat tools can be had for about half the price of the domestic hammers. Some imports are contracted to foreign manufacturers by American companies and could be expected to meet their high standards. If you decide to buy an import be sure the dealer will honor returns if the tool does not perform to expectations. Be especially critical when testing the sensitivity of the throttle: keep in mind that "almost as good" in the long run, is not good enough.

Figure 1.1. Two of my .401 hammers. The bottom tool is the older of the two. The upper hammer has a retainer with a bit inserted and a "snub" hose with a universal fitting designed to take up some of the vibration stress on the line. Both tools are equipped with the Industrial Standard air coupling.

Figure 1.2. A .498 shank hammer shown with its ball retainer off. As with the .401 hammer (Fig. 1.1) it is shown with a stress reducing "snub" hose. Note how the retainer when attached will add considerable length to the tool (and weight too!). However, it is an essential safety addition.

In the cyber world, you can use websites to do your tool shopping. eBay, for example, is handy for locating new and used tools. In this case, it is mandatory to know what you are looking for. Knowing the brand names, specifications, and model numbers of desirable tools is important. As examples, industrial quality tools manufactured by Chicago Pneumatic, Ingersoll Rand, Thor, Aero, Jiffy, and Sioux are good choices.

Tip: bid at the last possible minute for these tools; the market is fiercely competitive.

CAPACITY OF HAMMERS (BY SHANK DIAMETER)

.401 shank hammers. Usually called "riveting" hammer, they have $1/2$ inch to $9/16$ inch diameter bores and are commonly offered in one-to four inch stroke capacities.

The four inch stroke and $9/16$ inch diameter bore is the best choice for smithing applications. At this stroke they usually offer about 1600 BPM. Manufacturers rate this hammer as capable of cold setting $3/16$ inch steel rivets; I commonly hotset $1/4$ inch rivets with this tool. As I mentioned in the Introduction, this is the most used hand tool in my shop. It is used for center punching, line tracing for accurate hotcuts for hand or power hammer follow-up, deep incising both cold and hot on all metals, hot carving and detailing, riveting, repoussé on all sheet metals, punching and drifting small holes, texturing, peening and planishing, and slitting and cutting of light stock. All of this is accomplished with speed and accuracy. See the appropriate sections of this book for specific applications.

.498 shank hammers. This tool is a nice step up in power from the .401 hammer but still a manageable size. It has a $3/4$ inch bore and is offered in stroke lengths of from approximately $2\frac{1}{2}$ inch to 7 inch. Once again, the longest stroke is optimal. The 7 inch stroke tool has about 900 BPM and at about 6 pounds is almost twice as heavy as the .401 tool. Rated to cold set $5/16$ inch steel rivets, it will readily hot set $3/8$ inch steel rivets. It is best used for freehand hot work in steel where the .401 tool is too light for the job; it is used for larger carvings, cutting up to $5/16$ inch thick, hot slitting up to $1/2$ inch thick, hole punching, drifting, relief on light plate (including nonferrous), deeper incising, upsetting of bar ends and edges and, of course, riveting.

.680 shank hammers. Usually classified as chipping hammers, these tools may also be used for hot steel operations including riveting. They typically have a $1\frac{1}{8}$ inch bore and are available in 1 to 4 inch strokes. Once again, I recommend the longer stroke of 4 inches which will deliver about 1500 BPM (through a $\frac{1}{2}$ inch air line). This class of tool is also available with a .580 hexagonal shank which is designed to prevent the tool bit from rotating independent of the tool.

I have two of these hammers, one is a 3 inch stroke and the other is a 4 inch stroke, they are principally used for slitting. The round shank .680 is somewhat more versatile for smithing operations. Good throttling is essential. With this class of tool you will find yourself quickly out of control if you cannot "ease into" the work. Size and weight factor into the usefulness of this hammer. Weighing in at 15 pounds or more, manipulation and dexterity become somewhat challenged. With this in mind, I find this tool to be most useful for vertical down operations such as punching, drifting, lining, heavy texturing, cutting, edge and end upsetting on heavy stock, and riveting (I have hot set many $\frac{5}{8}$ inch rivets with this tool). Held horizontally, hot slitting steel bar or plate up to 1 inch when held securely in a heavy vice is much less awkward than the same operation done with a hand hammer driven hot cut.

1.217 shank hammers. These heavy duty riveting hammers are designed for hot setting $\frac{3}{4}$ inch to $1\frac{1}{8}$ inch rivets such as would be used on bridges and other massive structures when hydraulic riveting presses are impractical. I mention these only to fill in the category on hammers; their weight of up to 25 pounds makes them too unwieldy for any smithing application I can think of. Do I hear some macho smiths panting?

Figure 1.3. A relatively small .680 shank hammer with a smaller bore and stroke. This tool (shown without retainer) is under 12 inches in length and supplies the impact roughly comparable to my .498 shank hammer, with a more staccato pulse. Like all .680 shank tools, it requires a $\frac{1}{2}$ inch diameter air supply. This tool has a 3 inch stroke and for a .680 shank tool, a relatively small bore.

Figure 1.4. A "full size" .680 shank 4 inch stroke hammer with a $1\frac{1}{8}$ inch bore. Weighing in at 15+ pounds, it has the heft needed to drive heavy-duty hot cutting, upsetting, and riveting operations. It is shown dutifully "wearing" the ball type retainer designed for collared bits. These large hammers can become deadly without retainers; use them!

Figure 1.5. A .580 hex shank hammer with a screw on retainer which is integral to the assembly. A .580 hex shank tool is essentially the same as a .680 shank tool, just different bushings in the nose to match the .580 hex shank bits This hammer locks the bit in position preventing rotation. A handy feature for cutting and chipping.

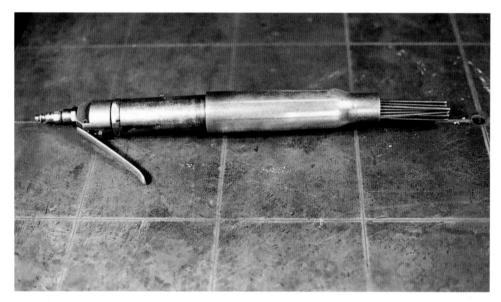

Figure 1.6. A flux chipper/scaler: Beyond their intended use these combination tools are very handy for texturing both as chisels or with the needle attachment (as shown). The one inch stroke, high BPM of this tool produces a superficial and rapid surface texture. Also use the needle attachments for blending welds into the parent material after first grinding flush; a very neat solution to soften the raw, ground surface. Planish with your .401 hammer with the appropriate bit for a really slick blending. Oh, also very handy for chipping welding flux and descaling.

RETAINERS FOR HAMMERS

Pneumatic hammers are capable of launching tool bits at a deadly velocity if the trigger is activated when the tool bit is unrestrained. For this reason retainers are a vital safety addition to your tools. There are several types of retainers for pneumatic hammers. The simplest and least costly for the smaller hammers is the "beehive" type retainer which is a springlike coil that screws onto the threaded front of the hammer and secures the shoulder on the tool bit. It resembles (you guessed it) a beehive in its configuration. These are the lightest and least intrusive retainers but usually require removal to change bits; this can be very awkward as you may need to use several different bits for an operation. Some manufacturers do offer coiled wire type "quick change" retainers but I personally find them impractical to use, especially if I have gloves on. The type of retainer I would recommend is called a "ball type safety retainer." It is available for the .401, .498, and .680 hammers. This type of retainer uses four spring loaded ball bearings that secure the shoulder of the hammer bit in place. Release or insertion of the bit is accomplished by pulling back a spring-loaded sleeve (similar in function to quick release air hose couplings). The only drawback to this system is that they protrude about an inch or more (depending on the size tool) beyond the front of the hammer. Using a standard length bit in this type retainer leaves insufficient room to hold and maneuver the bit, especially on hot work. This problem is eliminated by reforging of the bits which, as you will see in Chapter 2 of this book, "Design and Forging of Tool Bits for Pneumatic Hammers," is

necessary anyway. There are other retainer designs available for the .680 hammers, but in my opinion, they are not as efficient. Note: For the .680 hammer if you use the ball type retainer, it is necessary to use tool bits that are of the round shoulder design. The smaller .401 and .498 hammer bits are always supplied with round shoulders.

COUPLERS AND HOSES FOR THE PNEUMATIC HAMMERS

Whether you are setting up your air delivery system from scratch or need to accommodate a selection of hammers to an existing system it is prudent to make your choices of couplings and hoses based on function and safety. Interchangeability and ease of use are primary, especially working hot where time is always a factor. The coupler design that suits my needs is called "sleeve type, Industrial Interchange" that is the female half; the mating male half is unceremoniously called the "plug." They are available for all the hose and tool sizes used in this book (except the 1.217 shank size big gun). Operation is easy, with or without gloves, simply pull back on sleeve to connect or disconnect. There is a new version that requires only a push to connect, but I find it difficult to use if there is pressure in the line, especially on the $1/2$ inch hose. Lastly on the subject there is a connector that appears identical to the "Industrial Interchange" in a superficial way; but they are not compatible. The difference can be seen on the contour of the male plug. It is called an "automotive" connector. You might find it on a used tool that was used in an automotive shop.

Heavy duty Rubber Manufacturers Association (RMA), Class A Nitrile rubber tube reinforced with RMA, Class B braided covering is my choice for air hose. It is available in red or black from industrial suppliers in $1/4$ inch, $3/8$ inch and $1/2$ inch diameters. It is commonly available in 25 and 50 foot lengths with crimped National Pipe Thread (NPT) fittings.

There is a new development in air hose material technology that allows fittings to be inserted and retained without the use of crimped metal attachments. An appealing idea available at a considerable increase in cost per foot pricing.

LUBRICATION

Lubrication is an essential fact of life necessity with pneumatic tools. For performance as well as longevity, high quality, low viscosity, specially compounded oil is your tool's life blood. Deliver by a metered oiler mounted on the compressor air delivery system or an inline metered design mounted at the tool; the choice is yours. The alternative of a squirt of oil directly into the tool whenever the inspiration happens to strike usually results in underoiling or a sopping mess of overoiling. Do it right—save the inspirational moments for your art.

SUPPLIERS

To avoid the problems of trying to list suppliers of pneumatic tools in a thoroughly industrialized society in which sources abound, suffice it to say that they are represented ubiquitously on the internet under the heading "Pneumatic tools, industrial" and check the multitude of websites under manufacturers and suppliers as well as most phone books.

CHAPTER 2

THE DESIGN AND FORGING
////////////// Of Tool Bits For ///////////////
PNEUMATIC HAMMERS

If you contact your supplier and ask for "pneumatic tool bits" they will probably refer you to the guy around the block to get rid of you. In the industry what you want is called by the name "chisel blanks;" now you will get service. I call them "bits" for smithing applications because "chisel" is not an accurate description for most of the shapes you will need. So do not involve your supplier in a semantic debate, call the tool bits, for the sake of communication "chisel blanks." However, for my purposes in this book you will read "tool bits."

I have researched only to discover that there does not seem to be industry wide consensus for the alloy composition of tool bits for pneumatic hammers. However, industrial suppliers I have contacted all buy from Apex Tool Manufacturing. They exclusively use 9260 alloy steel for all bit sizes which is very similar in performance to the more expensive (because of certification and quality control standards) S4 tool steel. This is a tough, shock resistant alloy of the oil hardening type. From the beginning of my experimentation with pneumatic hammers I elected to use available blanks with preforged and machined shanks and shoulders rather than forging and machining the shank end myself. This choice was made to save time and tooling cost, assuming that I could forge the working end without annealing or distorting the shank. This technique has worked well for the .401 shank hammers. The .498 and .680 shank tools will sometimes require more extensive heat treatment. Using a technique similar to the quick method used for heat treating simple tools like cold chisels proved effective for smaller bits. I was able to avoid the sizing and machining of shanks that was better and less expensively accomplished by industrial suppliers.

SIZING TOOL BITS

.401 and .498 shank tool bit sizing. The first consideration is whether to buy pre-shaped bits to adapt for smithing needs or to forge all of your shapes from blanks. I would definitely recommend forging your needs from blanks where possible, for reasons you will understand as you labor your way through this section. "Chisel blanks," i.e. "bits," for the smaller riveting hammers are available in (respective to shank diameter) 6 inch and 8 inch sizes measured from shoulder to end. This size blank works well for most hot and cold uses when forged out to conform to my recommended configuration.

Figure 2.1. A variety of .401 bits for incising.

Figure 2.2. A variety of .401 tool bits for forming and punching.

Figure 2.3. Two long bits forged from about 12 inches of an 18 inch blank are shown here amid bits from 6 inch blanks. The second bit from the left is for deep incising and lining in hot metal, the one on the far right is for hot slitting. (Note the concave shaped cutting edge.)

Figure 2.1 and 2.2 show a variety of .401 tool bits. Figure 2.1 bits have tapered shafts for incising. Figure 2.2 bits are designed for forming. All the pictured tools are forged from the standard six inch blanks (shoulder to end). Some of the bits have been repeatedly reground, accounting for their shorter lengths. For some functions it is desirable to have more length than can be stretched out of this size blank. For longer applications an 18 inch long blank which is available for the .401 and .498 shank sizes may be used as stock; in this case cut off any excess length and save the cutoff for forging handheld tools. For most uses, I cut the 18 inch length down to 12 inches but you may wish to vary the length according to your specific use. The longer stock is handy for making hot-cuts, hot slitting and for other hot working applications. See Figure 2.3.

.680 shank tool bit sizing. Standard size 6 inch long blanks in this size are, in my opinion, too short for smithing applications when used with any of the retainers available; perhaps the only exception would be manufactured button head rivet sets. In the latter case, it is not necessary to hold the bit with the guide hand because it does not matter if the bit rotates while operating. It is possible for your supplier to order 12 inch long blanks (measured from shoulder to end). As I stated earlier, I recommend ordering your blanks with the round shoulder and using the ball type retainer for safe operation.

A worthwhile exception to my rejection of pre-manufactured bits is the available "bush" tool. For those of you who have never worked stone it has a massive end configuration that looks like a heavy duty meat tenderizer. I do not recommend upsetting a long blank to produce this shape bit in sizes over $1\frac{1}{4}$ inch because this alloy has a tendency to crack at the transition area on large upsets regardless of technique. They are available in end sizes up to 3 inches square. With the "tenderizer" teeth ground off they make excellent flatters or rounding tools for smoothing or texturing large surfaces of forgings or heavy non-ferrous sheet or plate or ferrous sheet. See the bit on the right side of Figure 2.4. Additional .680 bits are shown in Figure 2.5.

Figure 2.4. A variety of .680 bits. The two on the left are older shoulderless bits. Far left, a "star" drill for soft stone with a boss for rotation. The two on the right are newer shouldered bits. The one on the far right is described above as a "bush" tool.

Figure 2.5. Showing a variety of .680 bits for fullering, hot cutting, and slitting. Note the difference in the cutting edge design between the hot cutting (second bit from left) and hot slitting (center bit) tools. The slitter is self-centering for working on edge.

1.217 shank tool bits. As far as I know only rivet sets are available for this tool. It may be possible for your supplier to cajole a bit manufacturer into a special run of long blanks, but I do not know what you would do with them anyway. In this case, you are on your own.

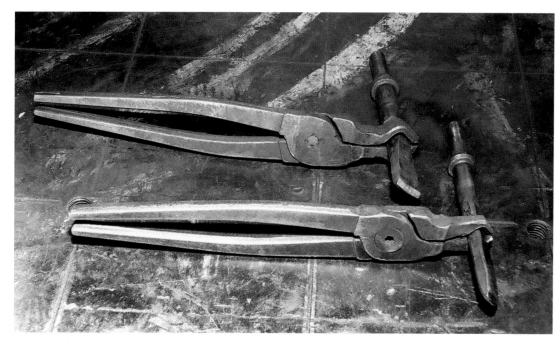

Figure 2.6. Tong-like pliers for holding bits is shown for .401 and .498 shank bits. The bits have a squared-off cross section through the middle.

Figure 2.7. The blank, ready to be upset, is mounted in the air hammer. Torch heat will now be used to bring the very end to a bright yellow.

Figure 2.8. The blank is being upset on the anvil. Note that this upset has been accomplished in one heat. Work quickly to keep the shank relatively cool.

DESIGN OF PNEUMATIC TOOL BITS

To suit my work habits there is an essential difference in my forging design of the bits for the .401 and .498 tools and the .680 tool. When using the standard length blanks I find the smaller diameter shafts, if left in their original round cross section, are too hard to hold during tight maneuvers; especially on hot work where your guide hand fingers are roasting right through your Kevlar (recommended) gloves! For greater control as well as comfort note the design of my tong/pliers for use with .401 and .498 bits shown in Figure 2.6.

By forging the length of shaft exposed below the retainer into a flat faceted cross section you accomplish two things: you provide a better gripping surface and you increase the length of the shaft to provide a little more distance from the hot work. Neat. Over time, I have refined my design of the .401 tool bits to a square cross section forged down to $3/8$ inch ($1/2$ inch for the .498 bits) of an inch square. A holding tool, shaped like a pair of pliers, was forged to accommodate the $3/8$ inch square shaft and the $1/2$ inch square shaft of the respective tool bit sizes.

This system allows me to work a little more comfortably on hot work and when a lot of tight curves are to be incised; the leverage that the holding tool provides and the comfortable handle pay dividends at the end of the day. Be sure to start your squaring operation just below the reach of the retainer to avoid binding in the retainer sleeve. This also allows a safety zone during your heating process to keep the shoulder and shank safe from annealing. When squaring, do not forge to sharp corners; this would make the shaft uncomfortable to hold. Forge just enough to create good, flat facets. If the tool you are making will need more mass at the business end, such as for a wide liner, rivet-set, or fullering tool, upset the end using your air hammer (Figures 2.7, 2.8, & 2.9) and then square off the shaft (Figure 2.10). Figures 2.11 and 2.12 address preliminary finishing of bits.

Note: If you are forging a hot cut or slitting tool, start with an 18 inch long bit cut down to about 12 inches, take your heat about half way up the length and draw a long taper. In the latter case, there is no need to square off the shaft first. This will create enough length to be reasonably comfortable for the guide hand during use and provide a good taper to reduce binding in the hot stock. The last forging operation is shaping the end to your requirements.

My .498 tool bits follow the same design features as the .401 bits, still retaining the square forged shanks, but shaped to $1/2$ inch square.

Note: If you are forging a rivet set or round punch it will not be necessary to do a squaring operation since free rotation of the bit during use is fine and the guide hand need not be exposed to prolonged heating because your guide hand can be located at the forward end of the hammer rather than on the tool bit.

.680 shank tool bits. As stated under "Sizing Tool Bits," I recommend using special order 12 inch long (measured from shoulder to forward end) tool blanks for this size hammer. Ordinarily this class of tool, because of its power, will be used by the smith for hot-work applications only. I have found the 12 inch blanks to be ideal for all tool shapes. Because of the increased gripping surface provided by the $3/4$ inch diameter blank shaft, I have found that forging to a square cross section is not necessary. This not only reduces the forging time but also means that less of the shaft requires a forging heat, reducing the risk of annealing the shoulder and shank. Of course, if you are making a punch other than round in cross section, forging up the shaft will still be necessary. As with the smaller bits you can increase the mass at the business end by using the air hammer (Figure 2.8) with tool bit inserted to do the upsetting. For hot cut and slitting chisels, start the taper about half way up the shaft. This will create enough length to be reasonably comfortable for the guide hand during use and provide a good taper to reduce binding in the hot stock.

Figure 2.9. Next the shank is squared up under the power hammer. Note the use of a $^3/_8$ inch shim on the lower power hammer die. Also note the tongs used to hold the bit have a heavy set of jaws as a heat sink to keep the bit's shank cool.

Figure 2.10. The squared up bit now reveals its intended purpose: a fullering bit takes form under the power hammer.

Figure 2.11. Forging completed, the bit gets a rough dressing down on the belt sander with an #80 grit aluminum oxide belt.

Figure 2.12. Continuing with the finishing process, the new fullering bit is refined with a #120 grit belt. This step is as far as the finishing process will go until the polishing following the heat treating described later in this chapter.

FORGING PNEUMATIC TOOL BITS

My method for forging tool bits is essentially the same for all sizes. However, the process I use varies somewhat between the smaller sizes and the larger sizes. To keep a sense of order in the text I will separate the process into two sections and ask you to bear the inevitable duplications for the sake of clarity. Note the process I usually use is not the full heat-treating method developed for this steel alloy which is more involved. It is instead a "quickie" method that I have had excellent results with but admittedly it relies on the skill of the practitioner to reproduce similar quality.

.401 shank and .498 shank tool bit forging. Bits with upset ends. First determine if you require greater mass at the end of your blank. If so, mount the blank in the hammer, then using an oxyacetylene torch set to a neutral flame, heat the end to a yellow-orange heat and using the pneumatic hammer, upset on your anvil. Be careful to avoid asymmetry and a multiple "lumping" effect that would create inconsistencies in the grain of the steel. If lopsided, correct before end is down to red. Reheat as necessary and repeat operation until sufficient mass is accumulated. If your upset results in a significant increase in mass, it can be difficult to keep the shank from overheating. If this results in annealing the shank, the entire bit must be heat treated, starting with a full annealing of the bit after forging by bringing the entire bit to a uniform bright red and cooling slowly in dry sand. Good incentive to be careful not to overheat shank and your hammer, if possible! Actually quenching the shank during this process may be necessary. Remove upset blank from the hammer as needed to quench. Keep the shank end below 400 F. Note the hardening, quenching, and tempering instructions that follows this section on forging.

Tapered and simple ended bits. If upsetting was not needed, the simplified process that avoids full annealing is easy to work. Heat the shaft about two-thirds its length while being held in your tongs and square-up under the power hammer or on the anvil (except for long hot cuts of slitting tools; see preceding section on design. Include the "business" end in this operation if you plan a narrow end, or not, if you need a full cross section end. If this operation is being done on the anvil instead of the power hammer, it will probably take several heats; cool the shank end with water as required. Do not quench the shaft down any further than is necessary to keep the shank cool. For your final forging operation reheat the forged end for about an inch and a half to bright red and shape to desired configuration. Keep that shank cool!

While still warm from the final forging, heat the end to bright red while staging the heat about half way up the shaft to prevent subsequent crystallization which would occur if the heat-transition is too abrupt. Now, while still showing color, plunge the entire bit straight down into a bucket of warm, dry sand, leaving the cooler shank exposed to ambient air. Leave undisturbed until cool. Proceed with hardening by bringing the business end of the tool to bright red being careful to avoid a sharp boundary between hot and cold. Plunge the bit straight down into warm oil. I suggest warming the oil prior to this operation by heating a piece of iron to color and dropping it into your oil bucket. After immersion swirl the bit around in the oil to dislodge air bubbles. Cover the oil bucket quickly with its metal lid to capture the resulting flare-up and smoke. Let cool. Remove from oil bucket, wipe dry, then power wire brush scale off down to bright steel in preparation for tempering.

Note: Be sure to read the alternative annealing instructions below regarding bits with upset ends. Those instructions require that a fully annealed bit also be fully hardened and tempered; recommended for bits that have a major transition in mass such as major upset ends.

.680 shank tool bit forging process. Basically the difference in my approach to forging the .680 shank bits from the smaller bits just described has to do with size and mass. Where I only use an oxyacetylene heat source for forging the smaller sizes, I prefer to use a small, tight coal fire for the .680 shank size. If you have only a gas fired forge or furnace and wish to use it, more care must be taken to insure that the shank is not annealed because the heat is slower and harder to concentrate.

If the "business" end of the bit must be upset to obtain more mass for your particular function, start here. If you are upsetting to make a rivet set, you may wish to use the shorter 8 inch standard blank, otherwise, use the recommended 12 inch blank. Prior to heating, if possible, insert your bit into the plugged-in hammer in order to save time. Heat the first $1^{1}/_{2}$ inches of the tool bit end to a bright orange color. With the bit inserted into the hammer, proceed by using the hammer's power to upset on the anvil. Check to avoid asymmetry of the developing "mushroom." Correct any asymmetry of the upset while still in a red heat. Repeat the process until you have enough mass to satisfy your purpose. Be careful to keep the shank below annealing temperature! For your final forging operation (or first if you did not need to upset) reheat the end for about $2^{1}/_{2}$ inches to bright orange and shape to desired configuration. If you are forging a hot cut or slitting tool, take your heat about half way up the shaft and hand or power hammer a taper down to about $^{3}/_{16}$ inch thick on the end; this should allow enough length (as previously described in the design section of this chapter.) Keep that shank below annealing temperature if possible. While still warm from the final forging, heat the end to bright red while staging the heat about half way up the tapered area of the shaft to prevent subsequent crystallization which would occur if the heat is not dispersed. Now plunge the entire bit straight down into a bucket of dry, warm sand, and, after it is cool, follow the hardening instructions for the smaller bits in previous paragraphs.

TEMPERING AND FINISHING TOOL BITS (All Sizes)

Rough finishing tool bits. Before tempering your newly hardened bits, shape the "business" ends to their final configuration. A stationary belt sander is my tool of choice for this operation but handheld grinders will suffice. Finish shaping with progressively finer grits down to about #320 grit. Keep in mind that the impressions made by your bits on your work will be only as good as your bit's finish. While at this stage of finishing check the shaft of the bits for a burr free and comfortable feel; dress down if necessary. Final polishing is reserved for after tempering. Note that for all size tool bits for the sake of expedience I have sometimes avoided the common heat-treating operations for tool steels up to this point. The tempering procedure that I use is also shortcut, but still requires careful attention.

Use a handheld torch for this operation. Oxyacetylene is what I use, but a lower heat output source such as fueled by Mapp or propane gas has some advantage because the lower heat discourages the tendency to rush this critical phase.

Hold the brightly wire brushed business end of the tool bit upright by the shank with close fitting bolt tongs (your heat sink). With the bit at the far edge of the feathered blue flame, work the heat slowly back and forth to half way up the tool's shaft but with the emphasis on the shaft. The point is to heat the shaft and have the color "run" down to the end. Rotate the tool as you heat to insure uniformity. What you are aiming for is a deep straw color right at the working end, quickly turning towards purple within a quarter to three-eighths of an inch, which in turn, blends into dark to light blue by the time it is two-thirds of the way up the shaft. If you do the heating slowly, the tempering colors can be controlled effectively. The shank should not show any radiant color at any time during this operation. When the right colors show, immediately quench in water. Now, if you have done a careful job, wire brush the tempering colors off and repeat the whole tempering operation! This is not an exercise in self-flagellation, it is insurance that your tempering is successful. In some ways it is more important that tool bits designed for cold work are more carefully tempered than those designed for hot work. My reasoning here is that hot work bits will inexorably require re-treating during their useful life because of heat

exposure, while bits used for cold work will work better throughout their life if properly treated the first time. Do not neglect to re-temper the shank if you had fully hardened the bit. Temper to a peacock purple running to light blue past the collar.

Final polishing of tool bits. After tempering polish your bits with a spiral sewn muslin buff loaded with fine carborundum buffing compound (black). A final buffing with chrome buffing compound (green) is desirable if the bits are to be used on non-ferrous cold work; this will provide a mirror finish and less frictional drag during use.

If your tempering is unsuccessful, particularly if the working end is light blue (annealed), the whole heat treating operation should be repeated, or to save time, just re-harden the working end and re-temper. If you are lucky your tool will not bust off part way up the shaft to expose big, fat, carbide crystals which indicated where a sharp temperature transition had existed at the time of the hardening quench. Actually, I have often re-hardened and re-tempered the ends of tool bits in exactly this manner (but carefully) after they became annealed from over zealous use on hot work. To date, I have lost only one. The alloy steel used for the tool bits is quite forgiving.

I have been surprised by the tool bit's resistance to losing temper during hot work; my theory is that the rapidity of the action creates a cooling movement of air between the bit and the work. Nevertheless, repeated quenching of the bit during hot work is necessary. Especially sensitive would be the hot cuts and slitting bits because of the low mass of the cutting edge coupled with the surround of hot steel.

Now that you have made some tooling it is time to apply these tools to the work at hand. That is, "testing your metal" both literally and figuratively. The techniques and methods explained in the following chapters are not arranged in a progressive order and should be used according to what projects you need to engage in your shop. My only caution would have to do with scale. Try smaller projects first to avoid the possibility of scrapping out a major piece of expensive material.

A SELECTION OF TOOL BIT DESIGNS AND THEIR USES

Throughout this book are references by number to the tool bit shapes used to perform specific functions. I recommend you use the following list, description, and illustrations of shapes to focus your energy on developing skills and tooling with the .401 diameter hammer before expanding applications to the larger hammers.

For your reference the following chart shows an assortment of tool bits that I find fundamental to marking, lining, incising, cutting, shaping, upsetting and carving of solid and sheet, ferrous and non-ferrous metals' shapes.

Most of these shapes will be readily recognized by the experienced hand-hammerin' smith. You will note that they all have multipurpose roles. Take a lesson from biology, that ultimate refiner of efficient systems: if a tool has only one specific function, the design is usually inadequately evolved.

TOOL BITS FOR HOT WORK (LONG SHAFT)

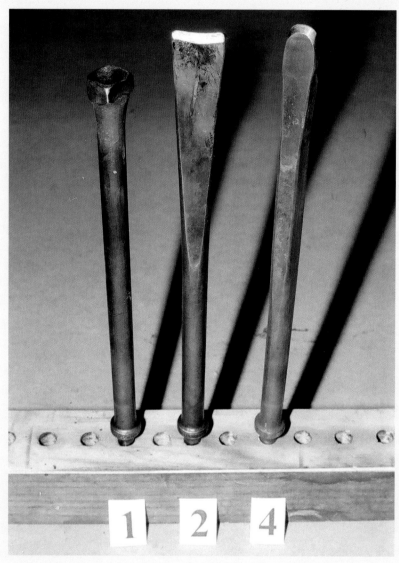

Figure 2.13.

Bit #1. Long "off square" flatter. Used for hot upsetting; the acute angled side is for working in corners (great for defining eye sockets). Shoulder to end length is 12 inches.

Bit #2. Long hot chisel, curved edged. For slitting or "peel" type cutting. Self centering cutting edge is easier to control than a straight edge cutter for its intended purpose. The length is intended to reduce discomfort from hot cutting.

Bit #4. Long 70° double bevel, narrow chisel. Used for hot wide and "crisp" deep incising in free flowing designs. Reason for length same as #2.

TOOL BITS FOR INCISING, CUTTING, AND LINING

Figure 2.14.

Bit #5. 70° double bevel, wide hot or cold chisel. For straight and gentle curve deep incising. Easy to "lead" because of width of blade. Also use for cold marking prior to hot work.

> Note: I do not recommend this or other bits of the 70° double bevel variety for non-ferrous sheet work because they tend to cut through or weaken the work by scoring. See #8 and #9 below for this function.

Bit #6. 70° double bevel hot or cold narrow chisel. Like #5 but for tighter curves. See note above. Also used for cold marking prior to hot work.

Bit #7. Cold chisel configuration. Normal cold chisel functions including rivet and light sheet cutting, removing weld spatter, etc.

Bit #8. Smooth radius (1/32nd), wide hot or cold liner. For shallow or deep straight or gentle curve lining. This is a good bit for clarifying lines, delineating design elements in non-ferrous repoussé veining leaf forms, and line tracing in thicker sheet work. Does not tend to cut sheet if reasonably careful.

Bit #9. Smooth radius (1/32nd) narrow hot or cold liner. Same as #8 but for tighter curves.

TOOL BITS FOR LINING AND FULLERING

Figure 2.15.

Bit #10. Narrow fuller. For wider lining, grooving, and fullering operations, hot or cold. This is a good bit for preliminary tracing of design lines in non-ferrous sheet. Easy line to refine.

Bit #11. Medium width fuller. Like #10 but wider. This bit is also useful for forming and planishing inside concave shapes.

Bit #12. Wide fuller. Used like #11 but wider yet.

Bit #13. Single bevel 70° hot or cold chisel. For raising a cut above mean surface. Nice for emphasizing depth of a cut by raising the cut edge above the surface plane. (See Chapter 4 for more on this). For safety, be sure to soften this raised cut edge by careful wire brushing.

This configuration is also preferred for line marking applications when using a straight edge guide because the flat side can be run along the guide edge accurately. A double bevel bit will tend to "wedge" the guide off the mark.

TOOL BITS FOR PUNCHING AND PLANISHING

Figure 2.16.

Bit #14. Point. For light or deep punching, hot or cold. This can also be your center punch, as well as your "nostril maker."

Bit #15. Peens 1 inch, $\frac{1}{2}$ inch, and $\frac{1}{4}$ inch radius . Used for peening and texturing operations hot or cold. The three bits to the right are great for forming and planishing concave shapes in non-ferrous sheet.

CORNER AND RADIUS TOOL BITS

Figure 2.17.

Bit #16. Off-set corner tool. As the name suggests, it is designed for refining corners in both hot and cold work on both solid and sheet. Handy on both animal and human features.

Bit #17. Radius tools, as many sizes as desired. These gouge shaped bits are used for any radius less than a full circle or for segments of free-form curves. They may be edged for a sharp cut or smooth 1/32nd radius (see #8 above). I sometimes reshape edges according to the operation performed. Used hot or cold, all metals.

RIVET SETS, GRAVERS, AND EMBOSSING TOOL BITS

Figure 2.18.

Bit #18. Rivet sets. Sizes for rivets from $1/8$ to $3/8$ inch diameter. Very useful for incising circular impressions. Hot or cold, all metals. Great for use in carving floral motifs. (See Chapter 7.)

Bit #19. Gouging bits. Shaped ends similar to hand hammer driven engraving tools but larger. Several different widths of cut can be forged and ground as needed. Unlike incising, which displaces material, gouging actually removes metal. I am impressed with how much control and speed the air hammer brings to all but very small cuts best left to hand engravings. For use cold on all metals, but may be useful hot too. Find the applications I have not thought of.

Bit #20. "V" or "U" bits. Great for embossing and stamping operations, sized and edged as needed. Example: one tool bit was used cold for the fish scales seen in Chapter 9, Figure 9.17. May also be used hot.

VEINING, FLATTER/PLANISHING, EYE TOOL, PUNCH AND ASSORTED TOOL BITS

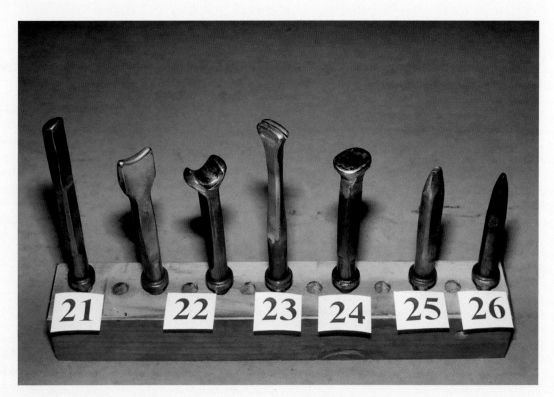

Figure 2.19.

Bit #21. Off-set single bevel bit. Used for undercuts to emphasize forms in sheet work.

Bit #22. Perpendicular concave bit. Used for raising or refining the edges of work in all metals, hot or cold.

Bit #23. Veining bit. Used for leaf veining or where a raised line is required. All metals, hot or cold.

Bit #24. Flatter. Used to smooth worked surfaces both hot and cold, all metals. Very useful for planishing convex surfaces.

Bit #25. "Eye" tool. Like a rivet set but eye shaped for animal carvings.

Bit #26. Punch. Very useful for punching small diameter holes or as a drift punch. These can be ordered as stock items.

TIME TO PUT THE TOOLS TO WORK!

CHAPTER 3

BASIC
'''''' Support *''''''*
EQUIPMENT

AIR COMPRESSOR

As you would expect, the compressor, the source of energy for your hammers, is at the top of the list as your primary support equipment. The optimum compressor I would recommend for a professional metal shop is factored by the number of people working there with air tools. For a one to three person shop a 5 hp, two-stage pump producing about 16 cubic feet per minute (CFM) @ 150 psi with an 80 gallon holding tank should work very well. The exceptions here are heavy duty high speed grinders which produce $1\frac{1}{2}$ to 4 hp but consume between 20 and 40 CFM @ 90 psi; that is a lot of air. These tools could be justified if you anticipate a high volume of heavy grinding by savings in operator fatigue because they weigh about half as much as comparable electric grinders. Usually this factors well only in very large industrial operations. If you are setting up your shop to include an array of pneumatic hand tools (see Chapter 12), calculate the CFM of the tools anticipated to be in use at one time to determine the size compressor required. Larger shops with more workers should have a proportionally higher output pump and storage tank.

The advantage of the two-stage pump is higher pressure storage. If you store air at 150 psi, the "free" air volume is 50% greater than if you stored air at 100 psi. Industrial plants sometimes have large single stage pumps that supply 100 psi (commonly air tools require 90 psi) on demand. One advantage of this system is eliminating the need for holding tanks since optimum pressure is immediately available. However, I think the 2-stage pump is more versatile for art metal shop needs and the storage capacity provided by the tank means line pressure variations caused by random periods of heavy consumption are reduced. If you can acquire a screw type pump instead of the common reciprocating piston pump, you will spare yourself a lot of noise; they are much quieter and more elegantly simple in design. And more expensive.

WORK TABLE

To adequately support pneumatic hammer techniques a good, well-sized steel plate topped work table is necessary (Figure 3.1). I suggest a one inch thick hot-rolled plate mounted on a vibration absorbing structural steel frame. If possible, a full plate 4 foot by 8 foot (or larger) would be useful if your work tends to be big. When ordering your plate, give your supplier your flatness specification to insure that they will check the plate for flatness prior to delivery. A realistic specification would be plus or minus $\frac{1}{16}$ inch per 8 linear feet. That degree of flatness will serve you well for layout and actual fabrication. The structural steel frame for the top plate should be proportionally heavy duty with $\frac{3}{4}$ inch or 1 inch diameter leveling screws on all legs. A flat and level table will be a tremendous shop asset which provides the three dimensional (length, width and height) platform for layout and fabrication of sculptural, decorative and architectural work. The well-supported steel plate is an excellent inertial mass (anvil) for pneumatic hammer back-up. Height of the work table is a very personal matter; generate your own dimension by holding your most used hammer with a mounted bit in the vertical down position. Your "driving" shoulder should be no higher than is comfortable and able to apply maximum power to your tool. This distance is important because your shoulder, for less strain, should be directly over the hand operating the hammer. Also consider how this position affects your back! My last suggestion for your table is that it provides at least an 8 inch overhang on all four sides to facilitate clamping.

Figure 3.1. My 8' x 4' x 1" thick hot rolled steel topped work table. Note the six leg design fitted with one inch diameter leveling screws. Storage shelf underneath displays my underlying organizational angst.

PLATEN TABLE

For heavy work in plate or solid stock a platen table, sometimes called an "acorn" table after a popular manufacturer, such as shown in Figures 3.6 and 3.7 is a great asset because of the clamping possibilities as well as for layout and its great inertial mass. My 5' x 5' x 4" thick platen weights about 3500 pounds plus the substantial mounting table supporting it. In my shop the platen table is positioned adjacent to the work table. The combined table surface facilitates work on large projects. Leveling screws bring the platen surface to exactly the same height as the work table in Figure 3.1.

Tabletip: Avoid welding fixtures and set-ups to your table surface; use clamps and hold-downs for securing your work. Saving that nice flat surface from grinder gouges and weldments will enhance your layout efficiency. It is enough that the soft hot roll plate will gradually develop a rich "patina" of dings which will serve as the history of your hopefully long and fruitful creative life.

CLAMPING HOLD DOWNS FOR WORK TABLES

Where "C" or toggle clamps work well for clamping to an edge, "hold downs" clamp work inboard on the work table plate. You may wish to fabricate my suggested "hold-down" design as shown in the drawing I offer (Figure 3.2). You will have to drill and tap ⅝-11 holes in strategic locations on your plate to facilitate their use (Figure 3.4). I used a six-inch on the square pattern of ⅝-11 tapped holes to assure complete spanning of the table top.

Note in Figure 3.4 how the ⅝ inch bolts are used to supply clamping pressure. The rear bolt rests on the surface and adjusts the clamping bar parallel to the tabletop, while the free sliding bolt is set in one of the tapped ⅝ inch holes and cinched down. This simple clamp can apply great pressure as evidenced by the flexing of the bars in the photo.

You will note that the screw size and stock dimensions for my hold-down design are heavy-duty. I do not recommend reducing the specified stock dimensions. You will find this tool easy to make and, in use, versatile and strong. Four "hold downs" should be plenty for most projects when used in conjunction with "C" clamps and/or toggle clamps.

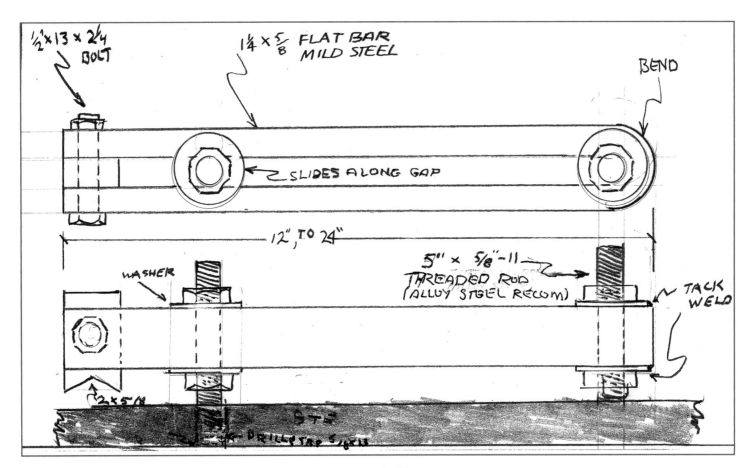

Figure 3.2. Hold down. Bolt at left slides along shaft and screws into work table.

Figure 3.3 Two "hold downs" of different lengths. For enhanced durability cut hold down screws from $^5/_8$ inch threaded rod available in alloy 4140.

Figure 3.4. Shows the use of the "hold downs" illustrated in Figures 3.2 and 3.3 to secure the inboard areas of panels being worked while toggle clamps are used on the outboard perimeters.

CLAMPING SYSTEMS FOR USE ON PLATEN TABLES

Spring type hold down "dogs". For platen tables heavy spring-friction type "hold downs" usually called "dogs," see Figures 3.5 & 3.6, are used for clamping heavy hot work with the pneumatic hammer because of the speed of application. I recommend using salvaged axles from pick-up trucks for hold downs. Heat the tapered end about half way down the length to a bright orange and starting at about one-third of the overall length, square off the axle and slightly increase the taper while breaking the corners. With a new localized heat, about two-fifths up the overall length, bend the bar to make a closed angle of about 75 degrees. Make the bend to about an eight inch radius. Now heat the tapered area to a bright red, place the bar in one of the square holes well inboard and hammer down the hot tapered area until the end is about flush with the table top.

Air cool the new hold down and test by attempting to clamp a piece of stock to the table. Just slide the hold down into position; it should "lock" on the stock. If it fails to "lock," check the angles, reheat as necessary until a friction locking is obtained. Then, and only then, is the hold down ready for an actual test. Cool the tool to ambient temperature in air, slide into a locking position on the selected stock, and "set" the hold down with a firm blow on top of the radius with an eight-pound sledge. There should be no rebound.

Rule of thumb: In order for the hold down to work, the blow that sets it in place must be heavier than the working blows that would dislodge it.

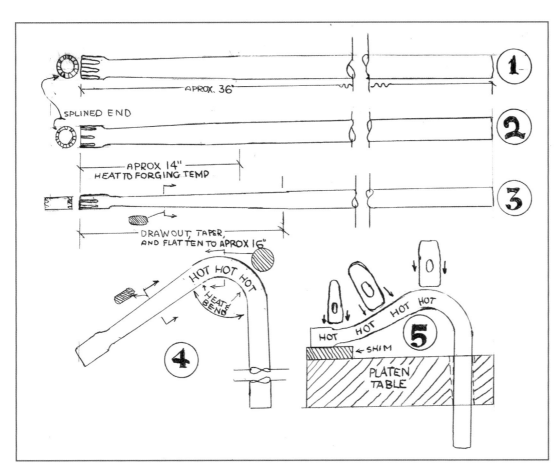

Figure 3.5. Drawing for development of spring hold down dogs made from axle shafts.

Figure 3.6. Hold down spring type "dogs" forged to the drawing shown in Figure 3.5.

Screw type hold downs for the platen table. The screw pressure type "hold-down" of the type I make for use on the platen table (see Figure 3.7) is also resistant to "walking" off the work. These tools utilize one inch diameter Acme threaded stock for the screws and "hold downs" hot forged out of one inch thick bar stock. Vibration is the key problem in clamping pneumatic hammer rendered metalwork; these "hold downs" do not vibrate. The primary disadvantages to this tool are slower setup time than spring "dogs," plus take downs require access to underside of platen to release cam.

Figure 3.7. Screw type hold downs work well but set-up time limits their utility. Under platen access is required to lock these shop–made tools in place. The addition of a spring to the pivoting cams could make these devices settable from the topside, making set-up much faster—try this on yours! Note that the "dogs" are cut from 1 inch stock and refined by forging.

Toggle clamps. These versatile tools have been ubiquitous in the industrial fabrication industries for many years but I have rarely seen them in artist-blacksmith shops. Made of forged steel with riveted joints, rapid action cam-locking, and without springs (which are susceptible to annealing on "locking plier" types), they are virtually indestructible except for the replaceable spindle screws. Simply adjust spindle screw to fit the assembly and squeeze handle to clamp. Available in several sizes, these are great for clamping sheet, plate, and bar assembly operations where modest clamping pressures are sufficient. Check out the photo showing several of many different types that are available (Figure 3.8). They be obtained from your local industrial supplier.

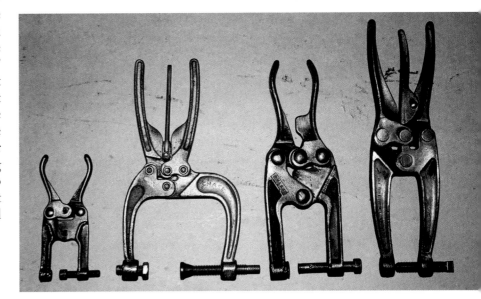

Figure 3.8. Toggle clamps. The two on the left are heavy duty (over 1,000 pounds clamping force); the two on the right are light duty (300 to 600 pounds clamping force).

"C" clamps. A brief comment about these most ubiquitous of clamping devices. They are available in all sizes and made with light duty cast iron or malleable iron frames or heavy-duty forged alloy grade steel frames. Only the forged alloy steel frame is worthy of the high stressed heavy-duty work done in a blacksmith shop. You will probably find many occasions, as I have, where you will need a "cheater" such as a bending fork to multiply the grip of even the heavy duty "C" clamps.

"F" shape slide adjusting clamps. Although these clamps are very easy and fast to use for welding and assembly of structures, I do not use them in applications where high vibration is a factor because of their tendency to "walk" under that type of load. "Walking" under heavy vibration is the result of the springiness that serves this clamp design so well in most other applications.

Hold down frames. Hold down frames aid in my approach to working non-ferrous sheet stock. The steel frames are composed of EOP (edge of part) bars. The term is used to designate the edge of a sheet metal part and is a widely used acronym in American aircraft and automobile industries during assembly. These steel frames surround the sheet stock periphery set-up for pneumatic hammer work and will maintain a flat base plane bordering the work. I cut 1" x $1/4$" mild steel bars to fit the edge of the part being formed.

Proportionally larger bars are used if the sheet stock being worked is steel or $3/16$ inch or heavier non-ferrous. The subject of working sheet stock is covered in Chapter 6, where the function of frames is discussed in detail.

VICES

A good vice is literally the foundation of a well controlled carving or other air hammer operation because of the vibration during rapid action. I personally use a massively supported large leg vice (Figure 3.9). Good luck finding one of these seven-inch wide jaw models, they are avidly sought and relatively scarce. You will note that my vice is mounted on webbed $3/4$ inch plate base, solidly welded to a segment of railroad track, supported under the pivot by 1 inch plate webs; and all this is anchor bolted to the floor. I modified this vice years ago to deal with the heavy hammer work necessary on large architectural pieces and massive sculptures. Well, it is also ideal for everything else including the handheld air hammer. Inertial mass is always a desirable feature in smithing activities. However, necessity always prevails; you should have good success using the more common smaller leg vices, or perhaps a large machinist vice or hydraulic vice assuming they are solidly mounted. Be thoughtful about determining the height at which you set your vice. If you use a blacksmith's leg vice, do not accept that the manufactured height is correct for you and your applications; these vices were designed as a compromise between hammer work and filing. Many hours were once spent filing; being closer to standing eye level helped blacksmith backs survive the tedium without the non-existent chiropractor. Today, (except in reproduction work), we use power tools. Your own height and work habits (hopefully good) should determine the best compromise.

STEEL SHOT FILLED BAGS

An essential tool used in this book is a thick cowhide leather bag filled with #8 buckshot. Used as backing, shot filled bags work on a displacement principle. Your sheet metal will mimic the shape of the tool displacing the shot filled bag. Very uniform soft shapes are thus made. Either steel or lead shot may be used with adherents to both types. Lead shot, however, will produce lead dust from the impact that will contaminate your air space. So steel shot is my choice. The selection of bag size and shape should be based on your needs. I have two bags, measuring sixteen by sixteen. They should be about two-thirds full of steel shot.

This size filled bag has a dead weight of about thirty pounds, making them also ideal for dead weighting assemblies to hold positions. It would be useful to have extra bags available for this purpose. To save on cost (and your strained back) some bags can be filled with clean, dry sand instead of steel shot.

Consider the tooling recommendations made in this chapter as personal choices based on my experience and work habits. I have provided my reasons for these choices where possible, but I encourage the search for alternate solutions to answer the tooling needs addressed here.

Figure 3.9. Leg or post vice modified for heavy work. Note the manner in which I transferred the impact shock of the hammer from the vice jaws to the base. Also, using a section of heavy rail welded integral with the vice effectively increases the inertial mass of the vice providing greater shock absorption and rigidity.

E.O.P. BARS

I use scrap steel or $1/4$ by 1 inch bars of mild steel and clamp them to the flat edges of a piece to be formed. This keeps the edges flat while working with the pneumatic hammer and makes a distortion-free assembly to its supporting structure possible. Industrial nomenclature uses the abbreviation E.O.P. to designate end of part so I call these perimeter bars E.O.P. bars. The bars of course can't be used while working on the raised side (flip side) of the piece.

CHAPTER 4

INCISING AND GOUGING FOR HOT HEAVY METALS;
Cold Marking For Hot Work

This subject is the first "applications" chapter because the techniques used herein are simplest to master, require the fewest tool bits, and are least likely to create scrap. The best configurations of tool bits for cold marking as shown in Chapter 2, Figures 2.13-2.19 are the 70° double bevel bits (#5 & #6), the 70° single bevel bit (#13), and the point or center punch (#14). The #13 is for use with a guide edge. The following instructions apply to all metals that are being prepared for hot work.

BASIC CONTROL OF THE PNEUMATIC HAMMER

"Drag" is the term I favor to describe the motion that I feel offers the most hammer control for traveling along a line. To assume this position the pneumatic hammer is held in a vertical down attitude and angled at approximately 80° to lead into the direction of movement (to the left for a right hander or to the right for a left hander). See Figures 4.1. and 4.1.1.

With this position your lead hand (the one holding the tool bit) both guides and "drags" the bit across the work surface. Meanwhile, your other hand is quite busy following along by maintaining the angle of the hammer and controlling the tool's throttle. Keep your body balanced with the hammer shoulder over the throttle hand while applying downward pressure. You should be standing slightly forward of the direction of travel for good control and visibility. Travel speed is determined by the "drag" hand based on the depth of the incise mark and the amount of throttle and downward hand pressure. Pressure, incidentally, should always be heavy enough to prevent the bit from "bouncing" which would result in losing control.

Figure 4.1.
Cold marking
with the drag
technique.

Figure 4.1.1 Drag technique. Your body acts like an anchor to control the hammer's travel along the line toward you.

Figure 4.1.2 Push technique. Your body's weight is inclined in the direction of your hammer's travel. It's good practice to use shorter "runs" to avoid getting out in front of your body's position and thus losing control of your hammer's travel.

"Push" is, of course, the complementary movement to "drag." There are times when "push" is the best position or the only possible position, or in some cases actually preferred. Extra caution is needed with this position since hammer control is impeded because your body will be out of balance with the tool leading you along. The likelihood of slipping off the line is greater in the push position because when you are leading into the work your body weight is behind the tool, whereas in the drag position, your body weight acts like an inertial damper and effectively controls the tool's forward progress. *This is very important!*

"Cold marking" prior to the hot forging operations of deep incising, splitting or hole punching is traditionally done with a hand hammer driven center punch by making a series of punch marks to delineate the cut, or singular center marks for holes. Using the .401 pneumatic hammer with the appropriate bits can provide a more easily followed, no guessing, layout for your hot work. It is fast too.

Marking Layout. Use a silver lead and holder (available from your welding supply dealer) for your cold layout. This mechanical drafting type pencil leaves a nice thin line that does not easily rub or flake off like a soapstone mark. I used to split the wood off silver "lead" pencils, carefully removing the lead and loading it in a drafting lead holder with a metal barrel. A metal-barreled lead holder is still preferable to the plastic type supplied with the silver leads. Try it, you will like it; it works much better for free-hand drawing than those flat "silver streak" holder devices used by many welders as a substitute for soap stone markers.

COLD MARKING PROCESS

First, a suggestion about hammer technique. Remember to "ease" into the work with your throttle while holding the bit firmly against the surface. Follow this procedure for all air hammer operations to avoid "walking" the bit off the mark and showering the work with unintended marks. Mark layout on plate, bar, or forged blank with silver pencil (described above) if you are working a dark metal, or, if you are working a light colored metal, use a very soft pencil or a black felt tip marker (Figure 4.2).

Clamp stock securely to steel plate table top or platen (see "Work Table" in Chapter 3). Avoid gaps between stock and table. If this is not possible on a forged blank because of a complex surface, use a piece of scrap shop plywood or a sand/shot bag as an interface. The objective is to dampen vibration that could interfere with hammer control. Distribute support of the work piece as uniformly as possible.

Figure 4.2. Marking layout.

Note: The common exception for supporting the work piece is during the rough forming of sheet stock, where to borrow an expression from German smiths, translates into "hammering in air."

Hole center marking is accomplished by mounting a .401 shank bit ground to a center-punch configuration in your hammer and punching center marks as needed. Here your advantage is a deeply marked, easy to see depression that is quickly wrought. For small diameter holes ($3/16$" or smaller) consider using a conventional center punch.

Line tracing for hot cutting or incising is a quick and very accurate preparation for the subsequent hot work. For this task you will need to mount a 70° cut or cold chisel configured tool bit in your .401 hammer (see Tool Bits, Figures 2.13-2.19). For a very visible hot working mark I prefer the 70° chisel. Instead of the traditional dotted or dashed line for your mark you will mark the entire cut by "dragging" the bit, under power, along the pencil marked line. The speed at which you "drag" your tool, along with how much throttle is applied, will determine how deep your mark is engraved on the work.

With the pneumatic hammer this full mark is rendered more quickly than a hand hammered series of marks. It is also much easier to follow this continuous and deeply marked line than anxiously searching for a "dot" while the heat of your work is rapidly radiating to your sweaty brow.

For long, straight line marking it is often advantageous to use a length of $1/4$ inch flat bar clamped to the work at the pencil line. Using the single cut 70° tool bit #13 (Figure 2.15) drag your tool along this guide bar being careful that your pencil mark is being followed. Now you have a continuous straight line that will lead to a clean and straight hot-cut. Figure 4.3 shows the guide bar in place for the straight line tracing. Figure 4.4 shows the line after tracing.

Line tracing curved lines, depending on the tightness of the curve, may require a narrower chisel configuration. Curved lines cut by the .401 hammer can be extremely smooth using the "drag" technique explained above.

A useful extension of this technique is to retrace the curves to increase the depth of the incision to create a surface design. If an even deeper incision is desired, retrace while the work is at a red heat. You will find this technique can develop surface design that is strong and showing raised edges (Figure 4.5). More on this later in the chapter.

Figure 4.3. Guide bar set up in place for tracing.

Figure 4.4. A marked line.

Figure 4.5. Increased depth of incision.

Tip: If you plan to hot-cut through on your incised line you should decide beforehand on the type of hot-cut desired (this also applies to punching holes): a. through-cut one side, b. almost through-cut with a slit finish cut, c. half way cut each side. If you opt for c., the cold marking should be incised on both sides of the bar or plate prior to hot work. The resulting clean cut is an aesthetic treat all by itself. The platen table surface may be protected by using "sacrifice" steel plates.

Perhaps by working with some of these techniques you have gained some insight into how the process naturally evolved from simple tasks such as marking to the more complex tasks of exploring the potential of the pneumatic technique for creative applications. Many possible applications are presented in the following chapters and many more await your innovation.

INCISING AND GOUGING FOR SURFACE DECORATION ON HEAVY METAL STOCK

Applications in this section evolved from the marking techniques developed above. Surface decoration on heavy stock using the .401 or the .498 hammers really opens up possibilities for surface treatment because of the control and speed offered by these tools. As stated in the introduction, the air hammer does not mimic the hand hammer; so tasks such as incising and gouging appear smoother than by hand hammer because of the rapidly delivered overlapping blows. If you are attempting to reproduce incising on period metalwork, the pneumatic hammer should not be used because the smooth cuts will be out of character. However, where period authenticity is not an issue, the air hammers potential can be a significant factor in deciding whether surface decoration fits your concept as well as your available timeframe.

SURFACE INCISING

After your design is traced cold (see Cold Marking), the options are to deepen the cut by retracing cold or by retracing hot. Cold incising will produce a sharper edged and shallower cut; working hot will produce a deeper and softer cut with subtly raised adjacent surfaces. See Figures 4.6 and 4.7. If you opt to work cold, one or two retracings will work-harden the steel or non-ferrous metal. Greater depth can be obtained by continued cold working if an annealing operation is included between tracings.

Tip: If you are doing a surface design with a shallow incision try using a tool bit shaped to a 60°-70° cut for your line (Chapter 2, Figure 2.14, bit #5 or #6) on plate or solid stock. For a different effect, use a bit with a $1/32$ radius edge (bit #8 or #9) for the entire tracing. Very smooth.

Figure 4.6. Incised line, two passes.

For all incising operations use the "drag" and "push" methods moving your bit along the line being developed. Maintain a slightly off perpendicular angle (about 80°) leading into the work; this angle, coupled with the proper contour of the bit, affords a controllable progression through the cut. Before starting the incise, position your body so that you will be balanced on both feet through the length of the movement; this will insure control throughout the tracing. Because of the travel distance of the bit it is difficult to re-balance yourself during a long, continuous tracing without affecting the quality of the line; exercise sensitive throttle control to blend an interrupted incise. Typical of any smithing operation, prepare yourself physically and mentally before a particular task is initiated. *Be in control!*

Tip: For an interesting variation on the incised cut, try the tool bit #13, Figure 2.15. The single cut edge will create a raised surface by under cutting that will emphasize the depth of the incise. See Figures 4.7 and 4.8.

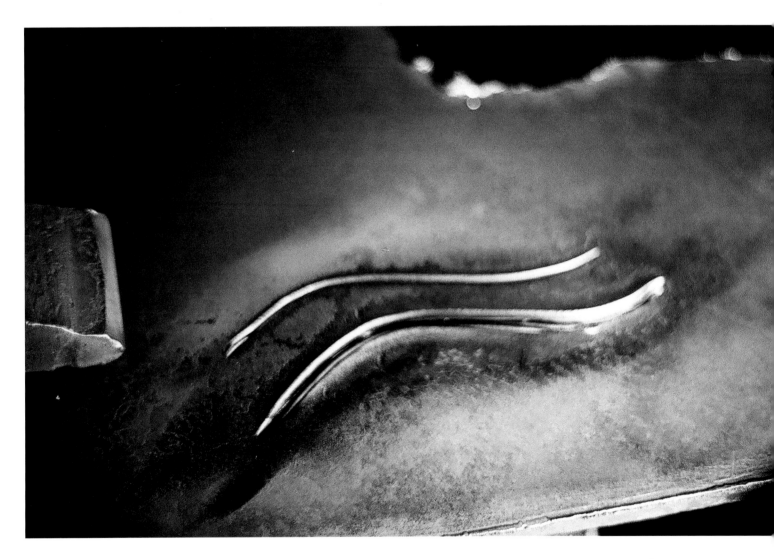

Figure 4.7. Lower line incised deeply, two passes cold, annealed, two more passes while still hot with the single edge 70° #13 bit. Note the raised edges. Upper line, two passes cold is a control reference.

Pursuing this move further on hot metal can result in deep under-cuts with beautifully raised sculptural edges, as seen in this detail of the relief from my sculpture "Where The Ancients Got It Wrong."

SURFACE GOUGING

As previously stated, this technique removes material, as opposed to incising, which displaces material. Gouging bits, such as bit #19, are limited to widths determined by the capacity of the hammer for which they are designed. For example, maximum cut-width for a .401 hammer will be around ⅛ inch. For larger hammers the usefulness of this type of bit is limited by the ability to maneuver the hammer through the desired design. I personally limit the application to the .401 hammer for decorative uses. Gouging bits tend to leave a micro-ragged cut; be sure to deburr by wire brushing for a flesh friendly surface. Lubrication with light oil is commonly used for hand engraving, which makes for smoother cutting, less resistance, and less sharpening of the tool. Oil can also help with pneumatic engraving for the same reasons. Cutting edges on gouge bits must be kept sharp for both controllability and safety. Gouging requires the hammer to be used in the "push" position because of the low angle of approach necessary to achieve the cut. Safety is also a factor in the choice of position because it drives the chip away from the operator. Proper body balance again, is very important; if your gouge bit slips out of the groove being cut, your body must still be stable to arrest the movement and avoid damage to the work. Engraving with the pneumatic hammer has not been well explored in my shop because I prefer the "look" that incising lends to the metal with the raised effect caused by displacing.

This is a technique that is waiting to be explored, maybe you are the one!

Figure 4.8. Deep undercut on "Where the Ancients Got It Wrong."

CHAPTER 5

CARVING HOT METALS
With The
PNEUMATIC HAMMER

This chapter's subject serves as an excellent example of the usefulness of the pneumatic hammer in the artist/blacksmith's shop. Using the .401 hammer for hot carving solid stock into animal and human figure heads and anatomical features can produce beautifully detailed work. Abstract and floral designs will be covered in a later chapter.

Before we put the hammer to metal, I would like to clarify a definition. Technically, this method is not "carving" perse, which is a "take away" process, such as in wood or stone "carving." It is also not a "modeling" technique such as in "built-up" clay or wax work. Instead it is its own genre, where you are disciplined to work with a finite quantity of material that you mold into what you envision. It requires good planning and visualization and an understanding of how the material displaces to make the form. That said, let's get on with the work at hand.

SOME THOUGHTS ON AIDS FOR PNEUMATIC CARVING

Vice block. I do not remember where I came across this block design but similar aides have been used by smiths for centuries to enable clamping bar-stock carvings at a good working angle. My vice block is somewhat more massive than most, using one inch stock for most critical surfaces (Figure 5.1). Lighter stock could be used but I cannot think of a good reason for such a choice.

Figure 5.1. The vice block. Note the heavy construction, particularly of the angled work plate. The lower part of the tool clamps in the vice along with the base of the carving.

HUMAN-LIKE FEATURES IN HOT METAL CARVING

"Human like" here means suggestive of human form. I do not aim for "naturalism," which in art-speak would mean the reproduction of naturally existing form, but rather the interpretation of the form for expressive purposes.

Blocking out the form. There probably are as many ways to "block out" a head in metal as there are creative smiths who have tackled this expressive task. I will illustrate this chapter with examples of some of my own head carvings; all completely detailed with the .401 hammer, and for continuity, illustrate the blocking out of these specific pieces. For example, Figure 5.3a and 5.3b show the block shape leading to a human head with featured hair. "Blocking out" should be accomplished with the power hammer or hand hammer and anvil. This is a good example of the complementary use of hand and pneumatics. Typically with these blocking out illustrations I spare the smith "how to" instructions on achieving this very basic form.

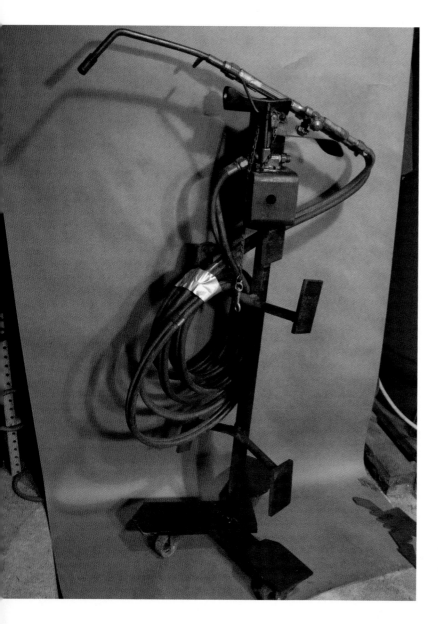

Figure 5.2. Oxyacetyene torch shut-off: I find it is most efficient to use localized heat for the more superficial carving applications. This device is an efficient way to keep your torch at the ready without keeping it wastefully burning. The built in off/on valves are activated by the weight of the torch and reignition is initiated by the pilot light.

"Walking" you through the carving of a head. Figures 5.3 through 5.9. These steps take us through the carving of a head with the .401 hammer and an assortment of tool bits. Note the point in the process where I switch from forge heat to torch heat. The stock is one-inch steel square bar. The sequence is taken from my sculpture "Where The Ancients Got It Wrong," 2006.

Figure 5.3a. Three quarter view.

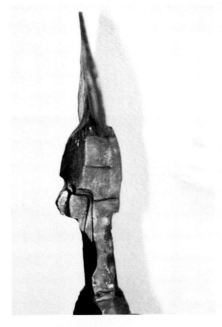

Figure 5.3b. Profile view.

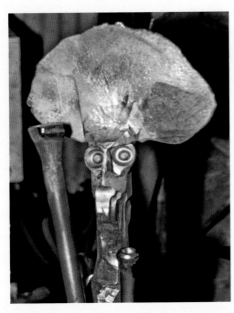

Figure 5.4. Forming the eye sockets with the flatter and punching the eyes with the rivet set. These operations are done with a full heat because a lot of metal must be displaced. Note that the flatter used is a long shaft tool to offer some relief from the forging heat.

Figure 5.5. The rest of the facial details and the bits used to make them: a medium gouge, a small gouge, a punch (for the mouth), and, not shown, a liner for the detail lines; all these moves were made with local torch heat or without heat.

Figure 5.6. The "hair" is drawn on the steel. The hair section is laid flat on the anvil or steel plate and, working without heat, the lines incised with a liner bit. On subsequent operations some of this lining will be obscured and will require recutting, so consider this an essential preliminary step to "stylize" the hair.

Figure 5.7. The hair is heated to a bright orange and hammered down to the top of the head. Use both a wooden mallet and, in selected areas, a lining bit. Drape the hair to your taste while working around the head.

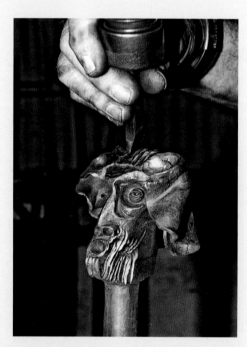

Figure 5.8. Once the "coiffure" is set the lining of the hair can be completed. This method of rendering provides a lot of latitude in determining the shape of the head by the drape of the hair.

Figure 5.9. Completed heads for "Where the Ancients Got It Wrong."

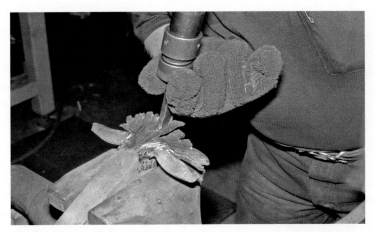

Figure 5.10 Head of a gargoyle. This shows splitting the drawn-out portion into tassels of hair while leaving some material for the creature's horns. In this manner it is possible to add complexity to the top of the head. When the "hair" is folded down over the head and the horns are drawn to a taper and twisted, the head will look as naturally coiffed as this fantasy can be.

Figure 5.11. More appendages (looking at the back of the head). The ears are carved out of the back of the head and the ear holes created to push out the ear form.

Figure 5.12. Looking at the face side the chin is drawn-out with the power hammer. This could also be accomplished by working on the edge of the anvil with a hand hammer. Note the eye sockets are ready for the eye punch.

Head of a gargoyle, Figures 5.10 through 5.14 are from a decorative piece titled "Hanging Gargoyle". Unlike the previous work this carving is one with the body. Since most of the torso is power hammer produced, it is not described here since I am focusing on the handheld hammer. The "blocking–out" of the head is basically the same as the previous head shown in Figures 5.3a and 5.3b.

Figure 5.13. Using the vice block as backup, the facial features, eyes, mouth, nostrils, and chin are punched. The resulting deformities surrounding the orifices provide a flesh-like naturalness to the carving. A hole is drilled and tapped ($1/4$ - 20) at the bottom of the mouth-hole for the tongue that is formed from a flattened $1/4$ inch lag screw with a threaded shoulder.

Figure 5.14. The finished head of a hanging gargoyle.

Note: That the lag bolt flattened tongue is installed and teeth have been created (which also locks the tongue in place to prevent loss). All the detailing has been rendered with the pneumatic hammer. The completed gargoyle is shown in the gallery section.

OTHER FAUNA AND THEIR FEATURES

Most other mammals share with the human the basic appendages and orifices that constitute our sensory equipment for dealing with the world we share; this includes eyes, ears, noses, and mouths, the features that concern us in the rendering of heads. The particular shapes of these features and their location on a specific species gives us the identity of the creature. It is not necessary for the purposes of this book to go step by step for every animal; it is sufficient to cover how characteristics are rendered that can apply to the general animal kingdom and let observation fill in the space.

Figure 5.15. Monkey figures from a tongue-in-cheek diorama using copper for the background foliage. All pneumatic hammer rendered except the basic body form. The bits used for the monkey faces were those used for comparable shapes on the human-like heads in preceding figures. It is immensely satisfying to me to bring these steel "faces" to life with expressive features.

Figure 5.16. A stylized chameleon, about 14 inches long, enhances the base of a floor lamp. Note the use of a rivet set to form the eye sockets and eyes. The body proportions and shapes that define the animal's nature must be in character if you wish to apply an outrageously exaggerated tail and still maintain an identity.

Hot carving, especially on heavier stock, with the .401 hammer is definitely a task for a gloved, tool bit guiding hand. I unequivocally recommend Kevlar synthetic fiber hot-mill type gloves. They are very durable, which offsets their relatively high price, and are excellent insulators. I personally prefer a full-cuffed glove as opposed to the knit cuff; they are easier to put on, provide greater protection for your forearms, and can be easily cast off if they get too hot.

Tip: Like cotton hot mill gloves, Kevlar gloves can be used dry or even wet. When your bit-guiding hand is working close to a hot mass of steel occasionally quenching your glove in water seems like a good idea. Be forewarned, however, that the water will be rapidly converted to steam by the metal's heat which, in turn, will tend to "cook" your hand to some extent. I often rapidly quench and keep on quenching during an involved carving. Once the glove is damp, you are committed to working with it that way until heat or time render it dry. Your choice, wet or dry. There have been some cautions expressed about Kevlar fibers. The EPA, to my knowledge, has not restricted its use, so I assume it is not in the same class of carcinogens as asbestos. To be vigilant about hazards to your health is more important than ever in this toxic laden world. So enjoy the benefits of Kevlar gloves, just don't breathe through them!

Figure 5.17. Detail from another floor lamp, this one using the elusive and secretive ferret to add an exotic note to the lamp base. Can you identify the bits used to make the animal's features? Take a careful look at the base disc of the lamp. The relief design is all .401 hammer work. Stock thickness is $3/8$ inch steel plate. .065 copper was used for the free standing leaves.

Mechanical descaling and cleaning. When the carving is completed, clean the work with a (preferably powered rotary) wire brush. The stiffness and configuration of the brush depends on the effect desired and the metal being worked; bronze requires a softer touch than steel, for example. Be sure to eliminate all unfriendly burrs and sharp edges from the work with the wire brush.

Tip: A very satiny finished surface on a steel carving can be rendered by power wire brushing the work starting at a dull red heat and continuing until cool. The brushing process can be concluded any time in the temper color cycle and the piece quickly quenched to retain a desired tint. Avoid obscuring carved details! Exercise restraint when hot wire brushing, especially when using an aggressive brush such as a stiff or twisted wire configuration.

CHAPTER 6

FORGING SHEET STEEL
And
PLATE STEEL WITH THE PNEUMATIC HAMMER

Sheet steel. The first project illustrated in this chapter, a decorative cap for a sliding fire curtain, utilized a .401, a .498, and a .680 hammer, the latter for heavy displacement and the former two for refining the design. The material was $\frac{1}{8}$ inch mild steel. I used a rose-bud torch using propane/oxygen with a gas saver for local heating. For the most part, I'll be "working in air" (without backing). Please note the frame design that I use for this kind of work: it consists of four pieces of channel iron that can be configured to a variety of sizes by staggering the channels. The steel sheet is tack welded to the channel sides about every 4 inches around the sides.

Before the sheet is attached to the frame, major lines are traced onto the steel surface to establish the major elements of the design. For this operation, the sheet is clamped down to my 1-inch thick steel table with a sandwiched $\frac{1}{2}$ inch thick layer of shop grade plywood as a cushion to allow the lining process to be easily seen from both sides of the sheet. The major lines are then incised into the sheet.

Use a rather soft radius bit, such as a #12 (see Chapter 2), because at this point the delineation is approximate and a sharper line could lead to cracks later on. This step is performed cold.

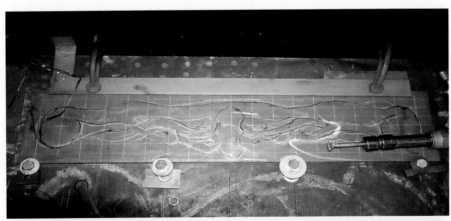

Figure 6.1. The initial lining is partially done. Note the use of clamps, bars, and hold-downs to keep the sheet perimeters flat.

Figure 6.2. The sheet, back side up, is then tack welded to the prefigured frame composed of the channels. As shown, an ample border was allowed for future trimming. One inch by quarter inch flat EOP bar has been welded to the upper leg of the channel to facilitate clamping and welding of the sheet to the channel.

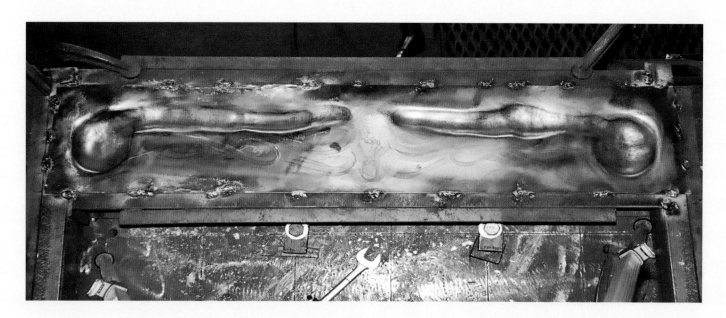

Figure 6.3. Shows the sinking of the forms using a .680 hammer with a 2 inch diameter radius bit. Note that the sinking should be done uniformly to reduce the risk of localized stretching. The tack welds securing the sheet to the frame are generous in size and frequency to avoid tearing the material. This phase of the work is done with localized torch heat starting at a bright red heat.

Figure 6.4. The primary forms complete, the piece is flipped, the edges are sharpened and the sinking of the secondary forms proceeds. As the heat is applied to the form, a working area is heated to a medium red and the forms are sunk. Hammer control is essential; quickly working the heated area while avoiding breaking through requires skill and concentration. Go easy until you get the "feel" of the metal. At this stage, the .680, .498, and the .401 hammers have all been used, depending on size of the area being worked.

Figure 6.5. The sheet has been removed from the channel frame. Work proceeds from both sides of the piece using primarily the .401 hammer to refine the form. Warpage is controlled by the table plane, wide steel perimeter of the piece and the use of steel shot bags when working from the back. Trimming the work to the intended size will be avoided until all the hammer work is complete. At this stage, all the refining work is done cold with the .401 hammer and the appropriate bits.

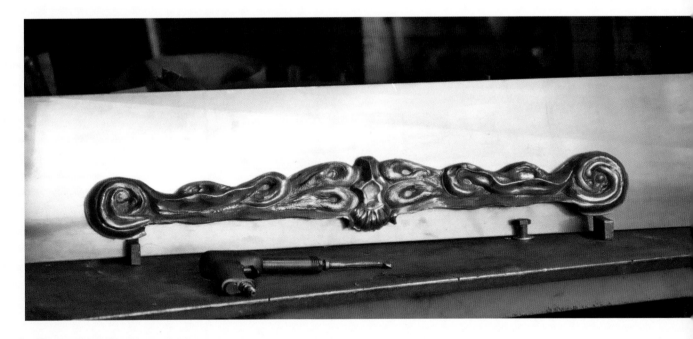

Figure 6.6. This decorative cap for a sliding fire screen has been trimmed to size with only minor work remaining.
Note my trusty .401 hammer — now at rest!

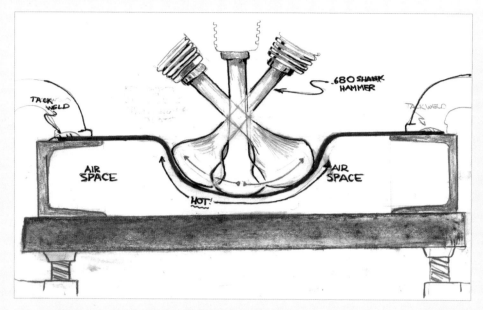

Figure 6.7. Shows the movement of the hammer bit to distribute the stretching of the sheet material. Tack welds prevent the material from shifting. Note that the heat is localized to prevent any dragging of the area you want to keep flat from becoming part of the "sink"; the high velocity of the air driven bit works in your favor to prevent this from happening.

Figures 6.7 through 6.9 show cross sections of a typical "sinking" operation progression.

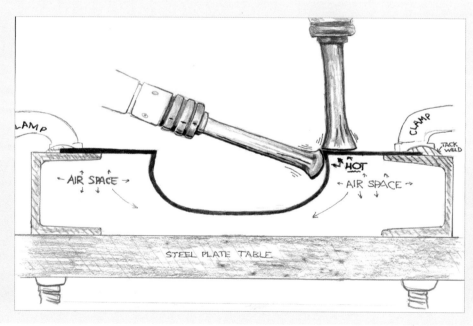

Figure 6.8. This illustration shows how a "sunk" form may be "sharpened" at the edges where it meets the flat. Working from both the inside of the sink and on the flat with a #15 large radius bit (see Chapter 2) will bring the metal together to create the sharp delineation. This action will, of course, broaden the sunk-in area, so plan ahead by making the initial sink slightly smaller. Be sure your objective is clear because this delineation will be near impossible to change.

Perhaps the most elegant feature of this method of working sheet steel is the simplicity of working without forms or any kind of backing and to still be able to produce complex, well crafted art or decorative pieces. This is because of the fundamental advantage of the pneumatic hammer: high velocity coupled with rapid blows. I can't emphasize this enough. The photo, Figure 6.10, of another piece I worked from $\frac{1}{8}$ inch thick mild steel sheet, a surround for a kitchen hood, is impressive for the depth of draw, particularly working with AA-37 commercial grade mild steel.

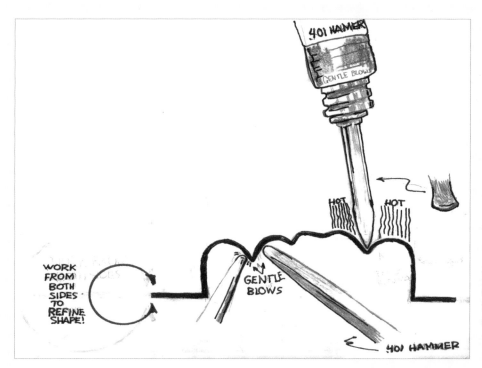

Figure 6.9. Taking Figure 6.8 further, to add detail in the sunk area, remove the sheet from the frame and work both sides of the sheet, hot and cold, as shown above.

Figure 6.10. A kitchen hood surround. Forged steel, wax finish. "Full Moon at High Tide." Note the depth of the draw, especially the moon form and the under-hammered wave crest; plain mild steel. All worked with the pneumatic hammer.

Plate steel. Creating forms in three dimensions can add considerable drama to what is essentially a two dimensional design such as gate or other shear panel configuration (see Chapter 8 for non-ferrous parallel ideas).

Three dimensional forms of sheet or plate steel can add a visually "weighty" mass and actually, if designed with the overall structure in mind, contribute to its strength. The stylized cougars designed to be part of my "Cats" gate have an aesthetic and structural role. Forged in sections from $1/4$ inch mild steel plate and welded into a unitized structure, the cougars had a strategic function as compression elements to mitigate shear forces at the upper corners of the gate. Their development sequence follows.

Figure 6.11. Drawn on the plywood, a full scale drawing in charcoal, the design is ready for tracing. Cardboard patterns will be developed at this point while visualizing both sides of each anatomical part.

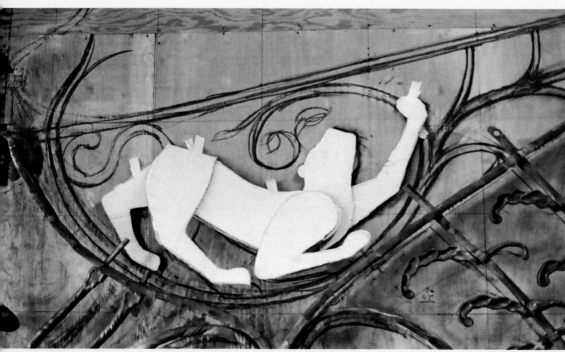

Figure 6.12. Development of the cardboard pattern is almost complete. Of course, it must "work" from both sides!

Figure 6.13. Tracing the pattern with soap stone on to the $^{1}/_{4}$ inch thick steel plate. Note how frugally the pattern is laid-out to reduce scrap. The parts will be cut out with an oxyacetylene torch. A plasma cutter would have been better.

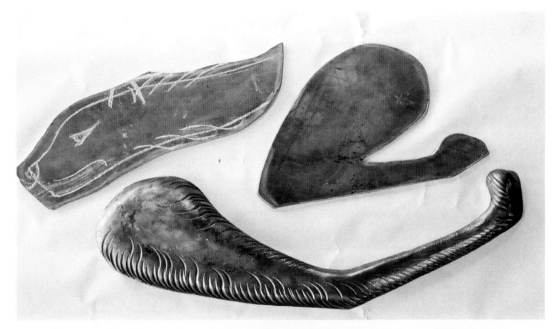

Figure 6.14. Various stages of detail completion. Half head is ready for the fire; a shoulder, partially formed over hardwood stump, worked by hand hammer, is ready for planishing with the pneumatic hammer on shot-filled bag. The other shoulder/leg is ready to be welded on the body. Note the deeply incised "fur."

Figure 6.15. More parts, mostly ready for assembly. Note the head and the partially assembled body. These collective parts make up a cougar, less tail. All shaping was accomplished by hand hammer over stump, followed by pneumatic hammer over shot filled bag; details have been wire brushed for photograph.

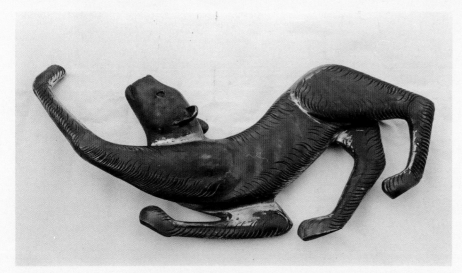

Figure 6.16. View of one side of the cougar welded together. Raw areas will be textured to blend with the "fur" coat of the finished sections. Welded seams will be undetectable on final visual inspection. The cat's tail is still not here mounted.

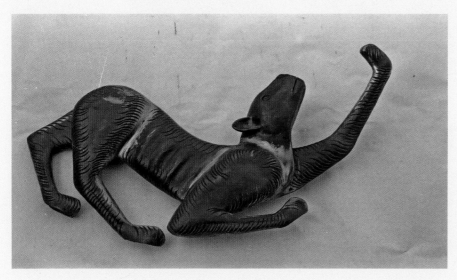

Figure 6.17. The other side of the cougar. Still no tail!

Figure 6.18. Here the cougar is being mounted in place.

Note: The wire binding the paws to the perch. Serving as a structural member, the tail partially seen in the upper left awaits final fitting. *The Cougar Gate* is shown in the gallery section.

CHAPTER 7

BOTANICAL THEMES
With The
PNEUMATIC HAMMER FORGED

FLORAL DESIGNS (FERROUS AND NON-FERROUS)

Floral designs can be elegantly rendered with the pneumatic hammer. Among the approaches possible, using an upset termination of a rod (such as a bolt head, or purely decorative piece) is very handy. There are no size limitations beyond the size of the upset. I use a bolt header to produce the up-sets up to about $1\frac{1}{2}$ inch from $\frac{3}{8}$ inch steel or non-ferrous rod (see Figure 7.2). Larger sizes are produced from larger diameter rod with the stem size drawn down under the hammer after the flower head is formed. The "bouquet" shown in the photo, Figure 7.1, gives you some idea of the variety possible based on similar themes, all rendered with the .401 hammer.

Figure 7.1. A bouquet of flowers.

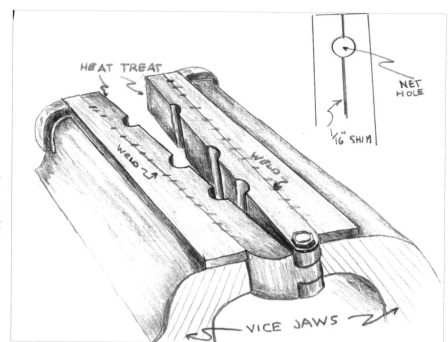

Figure 7.2. A design of a bolt header. This one has different size holes for several diameters of stock. The larger diameters are drilled on the side opposite the hinge for convenience. When drilling the holes, don't forget to shim first, otherwise the tool won't clamp!

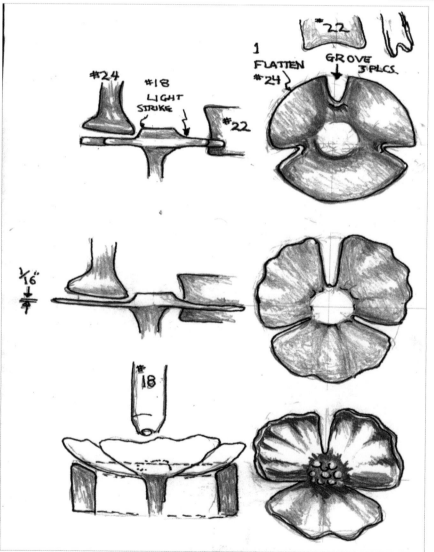

Figure 7.3. When the material is upset to the desired size, be sure you have enough thickness left to create the flower center. Using the right diameter #18 bit, lightly strike the center to fix its location. Proceed to flatten the area around the center to a minimum of $^1/_{16}$ then indent to separate the petals with a #22 bit. Finally sink the center with the #18 bit over a piece of pipe support tapered on the inside; this will, at the same time, define and shape the center of the flower. Texture the flower as desired. Try different size set bits for the flower center and various bits to sink the center and create a satisfying button shape. Texture as desired with light blows. The sequence of steps and choice of bits used above are merely employed to jump-start your introduction to this technique; explore and experiment, the possibilities are limitless.

The illustration in Figures 7.3 and 7.4 show the step-by-step development of several floral themes using the appropriate bits (see Chapter 2 to identify the bits used). To expedite producing these small "flowers" I use a small oxyacetylene torch and a "gas saver" fixture (Chapter 5, Figure 5.2 for photo and description). It is not necessary to heat the blank upset to bright yellow for most of the operations, a medium red will do nicely. For sharper incising and texturing operations heating to color may not even be necessary. Experiment for your particular applications.

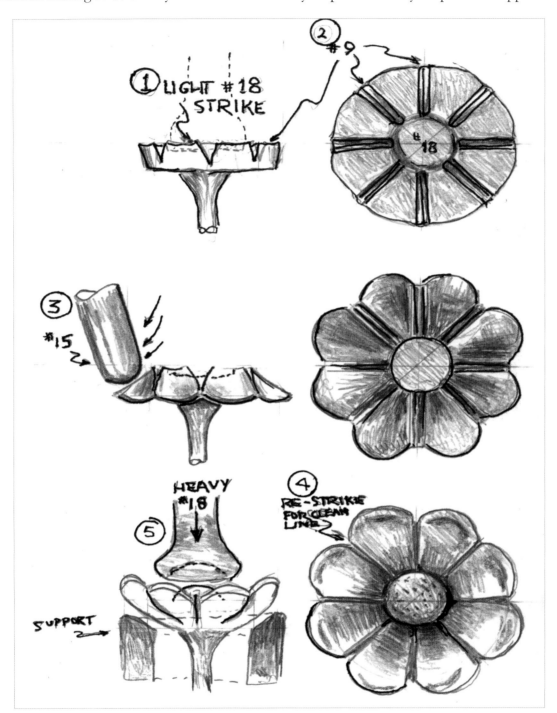

Figure 7.4. Illustrates a more complex multi-petal flower. First, find the center of the upset and lightly strike with a #18 bit; this sets the symmetry of the design. Then incise the petal arrangement as desired. Now draw out the individual petals with a #15 bit. Remove the forging from the bolt header and set it over an appropriately sized piece of steel pipe to support the flower. Using the same #18 bit used to strike the center, deliver enough heavy blows to form the button head and sink it.

ASSEMBLED FLORAL DESIGNS, NON FERROUS

Photographs below show several examples of non-ferrous flowers as used on my floor lamps.

Figure 7.5. Oriental poppy

Figure 7.6. Poinsettia

Figure 7.7. Wisteria blossoms

Figure 7.8. Magnolia

On the wisteria blossoms and magnolia flowers (Figures 7.7 and 7.8) high temperature acrylic paints were used for coloration; the type that is used for painting on glass and ceramics that is "dishwasher safe." This material is available in art supply stores in many colors. These acrylics require oven baking to give a glaze-like permanent finish. Follow the instructions on the containers carefully.

The copper poinsettia red leaves in Figure 7.6 were colored with high temperature glass enamel, and the green copper leaves were colored with chemical patina. Transparent dye was used to color the poppies in Figure 7.5.

In all cases presented here the flower petals were formed individually and assembled by brazing either with silver solder or brass rod. Both hand hammers (yes, I do use hand hammers too!) and pneumatic hammers were used for forming. The choice between the two techniques should never be based on dogma, but on what produces the best results, and if not that, at least the most expedient. To attach the assembled petals to the stem I prefer mechanical methods above using heat because, at this stage, I like to have the petals completely finished. Drilling and tapping the stem for an appropriately sized screw that would be silver soldered to the underside of the cap representing the flower's ovule works very well. See Figure 7.9 for a typical cross sectional view.

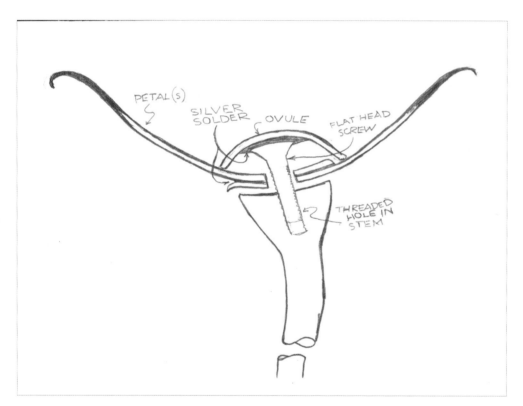

Figure 7.9. Illustrates a cross sectional view at the center of a flower with a screw soldered to the inside of a formed piece representing the ovule. I recommend the use of a stainless steel or brass screw for this assembly. A screw thread locking material such as "Loctite" may be used for final assembly, making flower to stem mating permanent.

LEAVES, GRASSES AND OTHER BOTANICAL FORMS RENDERED BY PNEUMATIC HAMMER

Leaf forms can be efficiently rendered in an aesthetically pleasing manner with the pneumatic hammer. The in-process photos shown in Figures 7.10 through 7.18 take you through a generic example of forming leaves.

Note: To prevent work hardening the lined indent, lining operations that are preliminary steps should always be struck over a soft substrate such as the plywood that I commonly use.

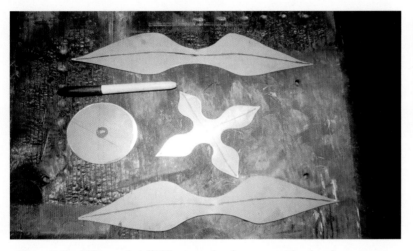

Figure 7.10. .062 annealed #110 copper has been cut with a bandsaw and placed on the work table over a sheet of 1/2 inch plywood. A center line has been drawn to locate the position of the leaf midrib (center vein). The leaf veins will also be drawn before the lining operation.

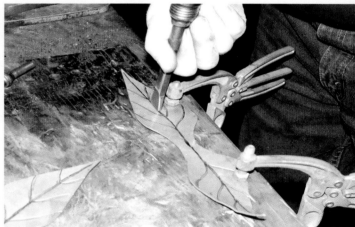

Figure 7.11. One of the leaves is shown clamped to the table as the midrib line is being lightly struck. Note the leaf at the left that already has the leaf veins struck.

Figure 7.12. Now that the mid lines are determined the leaf veins are lined in. Striking the midrib lines first insures that the vein lines are accurately placed. Here I am using a slightly wider fuller bit for the segments; the reason will become clear in the next figure.

Figure 7.13. Two leaf assemblies are shown here from opposite sides to clearly depict the accomplished lining. The tool below the leaves (see Figure 7.20) is for striking the midrib line. Note the soft edges of the tool and the taper of the groove that will provide a natural looking leaf.

Figure 7.14. Using a fuller bit approximately the same width as the median width of the leaf veining tool groove, line the midrib as the other end of the piece is being elevated by hand. Note the opposite hand supporting that end. In this particular case, it is what the design requires as the finished leaf resting to the left of the one in work shows.

Figure 7.15. As in the preceding figure, the quad leaf is being "ribbed" as the opposite end is elevated.

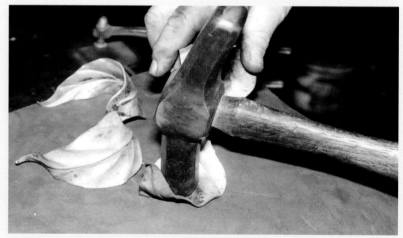

Figure 7.16. The effect of elevating the side opposite the ribbing process is here apparent; a cupped form results. This will be further enhanced in the next operation.

Figure 7.17. Yes, a handheld hammer! It is being used over a steel shot filled leather bag to finish shaping the leaf to suit the design requirements. The shot filled bag displaces the hammer's blow enough to shape the leaf without altering the lined veining previously applied.

Figure 7.18. Here the fitting together of the leaves is checked. The same process will be used on the "quad" leaf as shown above to form a cup to hold a candle for this candlestick as shown in the photo (Figure 7.19). The copper leaves will be patinaed and lacquered before final assembly.

Figure 7.19. Fully assembled candlestick. The steel portion (black) was forged on the power hammer, my Nazel 2-B. The base assembly was forged from .062 copper with the .401 pneumatic hammer. The drip cup was forged with the .401 hammer from .062 cartridge brass. All non-ferrous material was chemical patinaed and the steel stem was hot waxed.

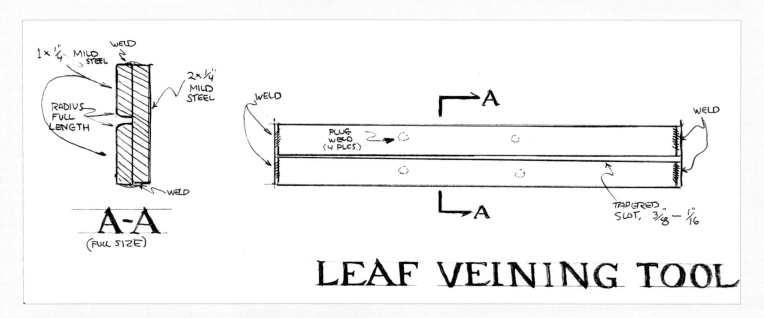

Figure 7.20. This simple tool will allow for forming well defined leaf veining as shown in Figures 7.11 through 7.14. For veining leaves of different sizes change the groove size accordingly.

A NOVEL METHOD FOR PRODUCING TAPERED FLORAL STEMS

Tapering floral stems of small diameters in naval brass and silicone bronze can be accomplished quickly by stretching rather than conventional forging techniques involving the hammer. I can only recommend these two alloys for this technique: naval brass, available conveniently from your welding supply dealer in diameters from $1/8$ to $3/8$ inch as uncoated "low fuming brass," and silicone bronze, #655, available sometimes from welding suppliers in the smaller diameters (used for TIG welding) or the non-ferrous suppliers in $3/16$ to $3/8$ inch diameters.

Figure 7.21. Clamped in stationary vice and locking pliers.

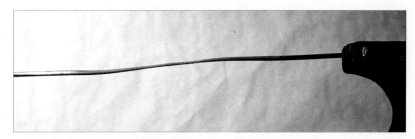

Figure 7.22. Stretching has begun. The locking pliers are now out of the picture frame. Note the thinning of the rod.

Figure 7.23. Stretching continues. A bark-like texture will develop from the stretching.

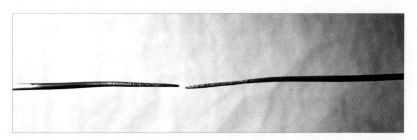

Figure 7.24. Stretched to breaking point. Result: two tapered stems.

Figure 7.25. An example of tapered stems silver soldered to the underside of leaves. In this case, rose leaves. The leaves themselves had been prepared with tapered midrib grooves using the leaf veining tool shown in Figure 7.20.

Great care must be used during the heating and pulling of the materials for this to work. Do expect to endure a learning curve to achieve success. Cut the chosen alloy to roughly produce two stem lengths; now, working with subdued lighting, clamp one end in a stationary vice and the other end in vice-grip type locking pliers, Figure 7.21. I recommend using some sort of hand rest for the pliers' side to maintain straight-line alignment during the pull. Using a small torch tip (about the size that would be appropriate for brazing) with your favored gas/oxygen system, carefully heat the entire length to be stretched by playing the neutrally adjusted flame back and forth along that length until a dull red is observed. Maintain tension at the pliers end to avoid sagging of the stem material. When temperature color is observed, begin pulling while maintaining a uniform heat. This is the trickiest part: how much pull, depends on rod diameter, the "feel" of the material being stretched, Figure 7.22, and the uniformity of the heat. And to complicate matters, slightly higher heat and greater pulling tension is necessary if your material is silicone bronze! This method of tapering stems may take a little time to learn but will produce a more graceful form and, if you look closely at the photos, observe the bark-like texture produced by the stretching. A bonus.

Figure 7.26. This photo shows the top side of the rose leaves from Figure 7.25. The stems are heavier than naturally occurring to prevent accidental damage to the piece. This is a concession I commonly make to the "real" world.

Figure 7.27. A longer leaf, this one from a poppy motif, better illustrates how the tapered stem fits cleanly into the tapered groove made by the veining tool.

CHAPTER 8

NON-FERROUS SHEET
⫻⫻⫻⫻⫻ Decorative ⫻⫻⫻⫻⫻
STRUCTURES

Kitchen Hoods

Fabricating large curvilinear structures would be difficult without mock-ups to guide progress. Working from two-dimensional drawings would be complete guesswork because you cannot build a three-dimensional shape from a two-dimensional drawing. The way around this conundrum is to use projected planes, which are based on the actual dimensions of the project, in a three-coordinate system. The three coordinates provide the three-dimensional method of measuring the project; they are named: the water line plane which is horizontal, the buttock line plane which is vertical along the length, and the station line plane which is vertical in the width – the station line is seen as slices perpendicular to the length. If the nomenclature sounds maritime, it is because it is! Historically, these terms come to us from boat building which was the earliest industry to build three-dimensional curvilinear structures from two-dimensional drawings. The water line, buttock line, station line intersecting geometry allows for projecting dimensions. This method is called "lofting" and has been understood for eons.

Lofting is the intermediate step between the drawing and the mock-up; it is where the station lines, working off the intersecting water and buttock lines, are strategically placed to supply the most contour information. Choose the high and low points along the longitudinal contour as the primary station line planes, and then as few planes as possible to control the curves along that contour. Do not overdo the station planes, use just enough to do the job; this is not intended to be a mock-up of a supersonic jet! Yes, the aerospace industry used this very same system for determining shapes.

Station planes, water planes and buttock planes intersecting each other establish points that when connected smoothly give you contours. See Figure 8.1. The closer together these lines are dimensioned, the greater the number of intersecting points will be created by these three planes, therefore, the greater the accuracy. These intersecting points, when connected sequentially in the third dimension become a "lofted" line.

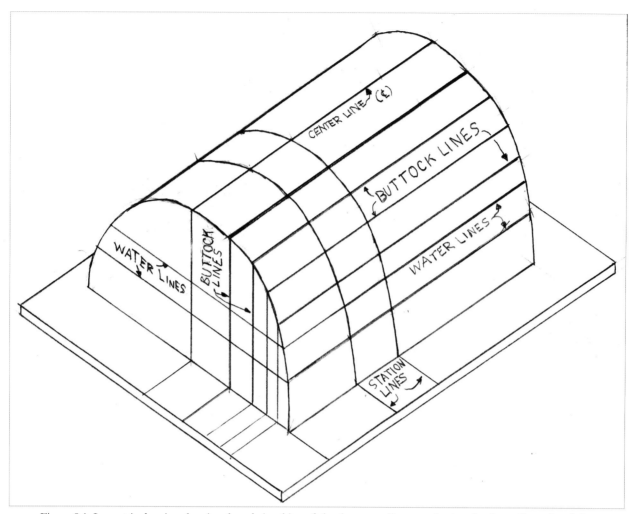

Figure 8.1. Isometric drawing showing the relationships of the three coordinate projection for three-dimensional shapes.

If the contour of the work is to be controlled, I strongly recommend using this system. Be sure that the station lines include the highest and lowest points along the length of the project. The degree of accuracy depends on how many intersecting planes are used to control the contour. Figure 8.2 illustrates how the three-coordinate system is applied to drawing of an object. In this case, I have used a shape made of flat planes to simplify the illustration of the method. Note how the water and buttock lines work together to define the station line contour (shown as the dashed line in the end view). Now visualize the same process working with a curvilinear shape...got it?

Brace between station plane contour panels solidly. Use 3/4 inch plywood for the entire mock-up. Use the base sheet (which would represent the wall) as waterline "0" and use the forward plywood bulkhead to represent station "0". The longitudinal centerline (of symmetry) represents buttock line "0" with buttock lines measured equidistantly from both sides of the "0". These measurement base lines allow for dimensions to be applied to the mock-up as needed. Use screws to erect the mock-up. I suggest using clear 3/4 inch plywood with waterproof glue; bracing should be 2x2s or 2x4s. When fabrication gets going your mock-up can be easily moved around the shop (see Figure 8.4) to free-up working space.

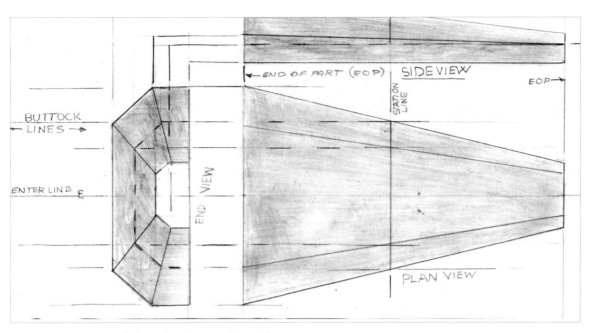

Figure 8.2. Drawing of object showing coordinated lines.

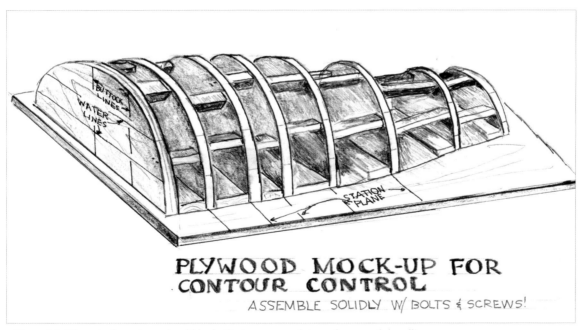

Figure 8.3. The actual mock up should be built strong enough to endure rough handling because it will be used for fitting, assembly drilling, and even some mallet work.

I prefer using .062 non-ferrous sheet stock for kitchen hoods. This heavy stock can produce very rigid self-supporting structures if properly designed. To succeed in producing a self-supporting structure it is essential that the internal flanges produced by joining the sheet sections are generous in size, or if a splice rib design is used, it has deep formed bead running throughout as in the hood shown in Figures 8.5 and 8.6. Splice ribs or flanges should be designed to be structurally positioned to resist twisting and bending forces. The bottom rail also has a significant role in supporting the hood.

Figure 8.4. Mock-up is shown moved out of the work area to allow fabrication to proceed.

HOODS OF SPLICE-RIB SUPPORTED DESIGN

The following series of photos details the steps taken to produce a kitchen hood consisting of copper panels joined by #655 silicone bronze splice ribs to create a rigid, self-supporting structure without interior bracing.

Usually, I choose copper for panels and .062 inch #655 bronze for rails and other high stress components because of its strength (and good looks).

Forming of panels begins with a mallet working annealed stock on wood forms. The mallet head choice is a matter of personal preference, as long as it is softer than the copper. A wood, rawhide or a "dead blow" mallet with a soft plastic face will do the job. If a "dead blow" mallet is your choice, care should be used to not over strike and cause unwanted localized dents in your piece. My personal choice is wood; specifically a section of an oak branch with the head formed from the "Y" portion where the grain of the wood runs in a random order. It will not split, as will even the best manufactured wooden mallets. Shape the handle to suit, make a few different mallets of different weights, face sizes and shapes. Enjoy a day in the woods while looking for the right down wood branches.

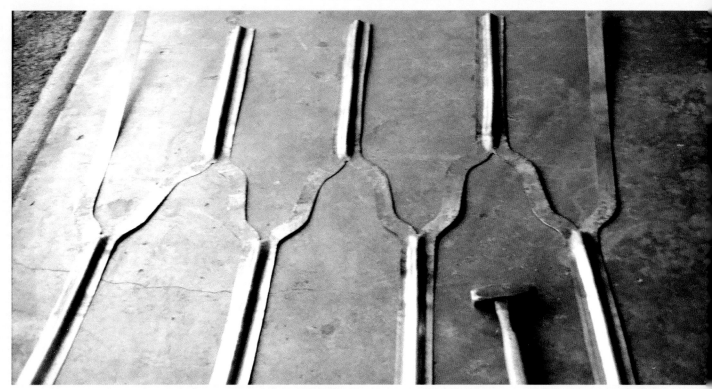

Figure 8.5. Here are the splice ribs (laid out on the floor) that support and space the panels of the hood. They have been band sawn from one piece of #655 and then spread apart by heating the unribbed areas.

Note: Since mallet and hand shaping does not alter the softness of annealed copper, it is good practice to finish the forming with a planishing operation to harden the material. A planishing bit mounted in a pneumatic hammer or a light hand hammer with proper back-up will work. Handheld "dollies," such as used in auto body work, or an improvised piece of scrap steel will do as a handheld "anvil."

Shaping can best be done on wood forms with concave and convex sides. These forms do not have to match the contours you ultimately are planning to render; just moving the metal in the right direction is fine. Some shaping may be accomplished simply by manipulating the annealed sheet with hand pressure.

Commercially built planishing machines are available which operate on pneumatic pressure. Essentially, the machine consists of a pneumatic hammer barrel (sans handle) with a .401 shanked planishing bit mounted solidly on a vertically adjustable carriage above an interchangeable anvil of various radii. This machine is usually controlled by a foot-operated pneumatic valve allowing two hands to handle the work. Usually, the machine is built with a deep throat to enable passage of large sheets.

Anneal all non-ferrous stock by torch to a dull red and water quench before working.

Note: Since #655 silicone bronze components are workable hot, the quench operation may be skipped if major displacement during hammer forming is planned.

For hood assemblies because of the large number of clecos required to hold the pieces to be joined snugly together, I prefer using just the 1/8 inch shank size clecos. If the piece requires larger diameter rivets, simply drill out the holes to the larger size as assembly progresses while maintaining alignment with clecos in the yet to be enlarged holes. Or, buy clecos for the size rivets required.

Riveting the hood together. For the exposed rib splice joinery of this type of kitchen hood I prefer 1/8 inch diameter button head brass rivets and plenty of them. Setting these small diameter rivets with a pneumatic hammer is fast work with a bucking bar with or without a helper. Two times the diameter (or even slightly less) is plenty of "head" to give you a tight joint. Use the same drill size as the rivet body size. One to 1 1/2 inch rivet spacing is adequate and provides a nice decorative touch as well. Use a flat bucking bar and a close fitting rivet set in your hammer. Work down the hole pattern by replacing a cleco with a rivet as you go. Do not try to skip around the hole pattern; "cleco" every hole in the row that is in work and remove them only to be replaced by a rivet.

Figure 8.6. Using the mock-up as an assembly fixture, the splice ribs are positioned in place and mallet hammered to conform to the contour. As the fitting proceeds, toggle clamps are used to secure the ribs to the station planes. The mock-up has been upended for a visual check and for this photo.

Figure 8.7. Wood forms used for shaping the annealed copper panels. In this case the forms include all the shaping necessary for each of the lower segments of the hood except for some compound contour work on the far end that must be done with steel hammer and "dolly."

Figure 8.8. Using the mock-up as a check and assembly fixture. Note the use of toggle clamps to hold the parts in place in preparation for drilling the pilot holes for the clecos.

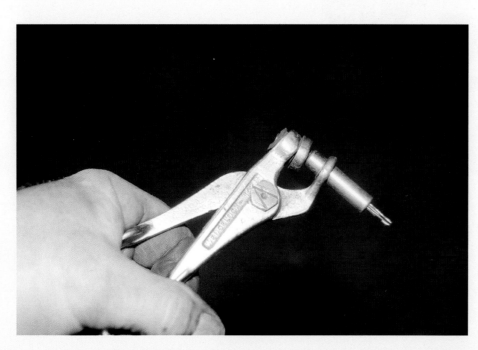

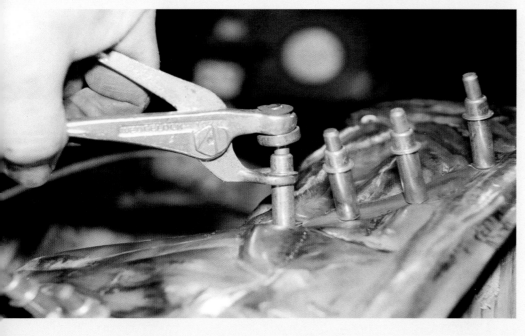

Figure 8.9. Clecos and the special pliers required to install them. Long used in industrial sheet metal fabrication, this tool is used to great advantage by craftspeople for the same applications; holding sheet metal assemblies together for riveting. The plunger is pressed down by the plier extending the split nosepiece past a tapered center pin, thereby reducing its outer diameter. The nosepiece is then inserted in the pre-drilled hole and the pliers are then released to allow the split pin to retract. The work is now firmly clamped together through the drilled hole.

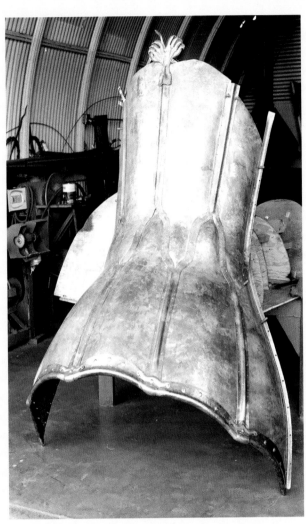

Figure 8.10. The partially assembled hood, held together with clecos, toggle clamps, and some of the permanently installed rivets. Note how rigid the assembly already is; particularly with the #655 silicone bronze lower rail in place. The upper rail has not been finished at this point and is not shown.

Figure 8.11. The completed and installed rib-spliced constructed kitchen hood. Note the solid and substantial feeling of this frame-less design and the ripple and wave free surface of the copper clad backboard.

USING FLANGES TO REINFORCE A STRUCTURE

Internal or external flanges created from the panels themselves may be used instead of, or in addition to, splice ribs to rigidify a structure. The photo in Figure 8.12 shows a detail of another hood where I employed internal and external flanges as well as splice ribs to achieve a viable structure. In this case, the variety of structural choices contributed to the aesthetic success of the work.

Figure 8.12. Notice on this kitchen hood the application of external splice ribs and internal and external flanges. Notice also the decorative floral motifs just for the fun of it! The entire wall side of the hood is flanged and attached to the backboard explained in this chapter.

TYPES OF SPLICES—CONNECTING THE PIECES TO MAKE A WHOLE

The bottom rail or surround. The bottom rail or surround, structurally, the most significant lateral member of the hood, is also of aesthetically equal importance — closest to the eye and hand, and often conveying thematic importance; it literally "stands out" and is not to be neglected. The following series of photos, Figures 8.14 through 8.20, shows and describes the development of one kitchen hood rail rendered in #655 silicone bronze.

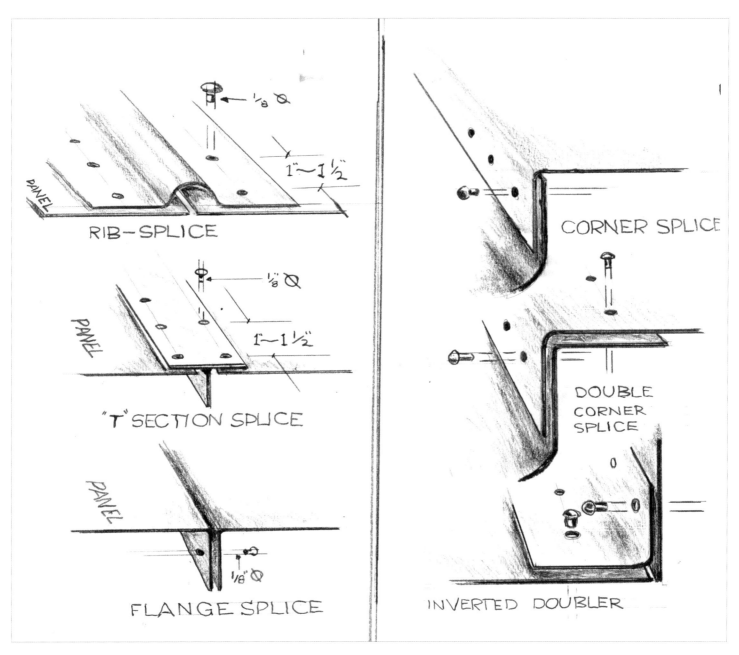

RIB–SPLICE

"T" SECTION SPLICE

FLANGE SPLICE

CORNER SPLICE

DOUBLE CORNER SPLICE

INVERTED DOUBLER

Figure 8.13. Drawing illustrates the types of splices used in this chapter.

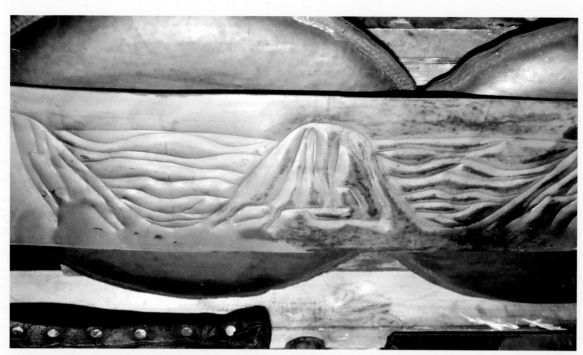

Figure 8.14. The loose pattern of coastal mountains and ocean motif has been lined onto the #655 rail stock. Now the work will proceed on the flip side to enhance the image.

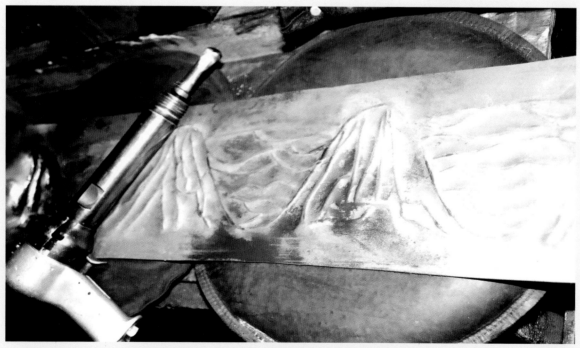

Figure 8.15. Shaping the rail progresses from the back side. Since all the hammer work is being done at room temperature on the .062 thick silicone bronze, a long stroke .498 hammer is being used to move the annealed but still stubborn metal. It is being worked over two 50# steel-shot filled bags.

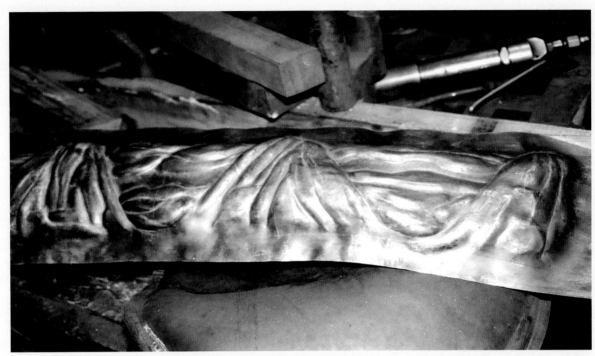

Figure 8.16. This rail segment is now ready for lower bead which will act as a stiffener and tend to take out the naturally occurring curve seen here. After beading the piece will be annealed.

Figure 8.17. Softened by annealing, the segment is curved to match the contour of the mock-up template by hammering it with a heavy rawhide mallet over a wooden form. This operation requires careful monitoring.

Figure 8.18. The fitting operation with the three segments that comprise the rail is underway with the match-up almost complete.

Figure 8.19. Coordinating the rail with the major front panel and the longitudinal splices is next.

Figure 8.20. Fitting the lower end of the splice over the segments of the rail requires a fistful of clecos to hold the members together. Rivets will replace the clecos one at a time.

Note: The hood shown detailed in Figures 8.14 through 8.20 is not shown complete in this book.

The backboard. In most cases a kitchen hood should have a backboard unless the surface above the stove has been previously finished in tile or some other durable material. I prefer using 1-inch thick clear plywood. To this plywood sheet bond a .032 facing of copper with contact cement. This is very tricky process that requires some finesse.

1. Cut the plywood to the same size as the back silhouette of the hood, leave about $1/4$ inch clearance on the sides. At this time, make the appropriate cutouts for the necessary ducting if required. Sand lightly to remove all traces of contamination, including fingerprints. Dust.

2. Cut the copper sheet generously oversize and degrease thoroughly on side to be bonded with lacquer thinner or acetone. Use respirator. Set aside and keep dust free.

3. Coat both surfaces to be bonded with adhesive and let dry (follow instructions from manufacturer).

4. Apply copper to plywood matching edges exactly. Do not attempt to realign once initial contact is made, the copper sheet will be ruined. Upon successfully bonding the copper facing to plywood use a roller to insure full contact. The appearance should be smooth and ripple free.

5. Fit the sheathed backboard to the hood either before or during installation.

Before proceeding with my backboard procedure check this cautionary tale.

It is imperative that local, regional, and/or state fire regulations be checked for restrictions on materials acceptable to be used in back of, or on the wall above, kitchen stoves. Some regulations may require surfaces or backing such as fire resistant gypsum or cement board complete with insulated fasteners. If these regulations exist, see if the backboard can be added over the required firewall. If this option is acceptable, it could be possible to reduce the backboard thickness to $1/2$ to $5/8$ inch for the plywood layer.

Finish or not? Whether to apply a finish to a completed kitchen hood deserves some thought. Kitchen hoods are decorative only secondarily, no matter how extravagantly built. Their primary role is to route grease laden smoke and moisture out of the room. Frequent cleanings would tend to unevenly wear through a hard coating such as lacquer and eventually be spotty and uneven in appearance. It may be best to settle initially for a paste wax finish and let the normal maintenance determine the hood's finish. An occasional cleaning with a good brass polish should enhance the "patina" admirably.

Figure 8.21. Full image of the hood detail in Figure 8.12. This hood measures nine feet wide, spanning a double commercial size range.

CHAPTER 9

ADDING MASS
To
LINEAR DESIGNS

It can be aesthetically pleasing to add some visual mass to linear designs, thereby lending variety to the size of the elements included in the composition. Often the elements that appear greatest in volume are also most conspicuously carrying the brunt of the thematic content of the design.

There is also a mundane aspect to add to the reasoning; since mass takes up space, it can reduce the need for forging a bunch of linear details that would be needed to fill that same space. Perhaps the most relevant example of "space-filling" exists in building codes that specify maximum allowable openings in architectural hardware to protect toddlers from willful experimentation with free-fall. That said, it can be practical to add some well conceived pneumatic hammered ferrous or non-ferrous sheet to your linear designs!

Introducing panels into linear designs. Selecting the material for panels has aesthetic and practical consequences. If the possibilities for adding mass are considered abstractly, plastics, stone, glass, shells, etc., are all candidates to expand the palette, and have been used to great effect by me and many others. For this book, however, technique will limit our option to metals. Considering cost is a good place to begin. Steel would cost less than non-ferrous and has better mechanical properties (if that is a factor), but actually could be considerably more expensive to produce because much of the forming needs to be done hot (see Chapter 6, Forging Sheet Steel). Copper and bronze elements are usually worked in an annealed state, meaning that they are worked at ambient temperature which can cost less in process to form with the pneumatic hammer than comparable sheet steel parts. Most of the panel work illustrated in the sequential photos in this chapter are either copper or silicone bronze and, aside from being self supporting, none are essential to the shear panel function of the steel structure they occupy.

Basic forming procedure. The illustrations in Figures 9.1 through 9.8 show the basic step-by-step process used to form panels. For the sake of simplicity, a plan view is not shown for the hypothetical panel in this sequence. The panel would be clamped around the entire perimeter, not just on two sides.

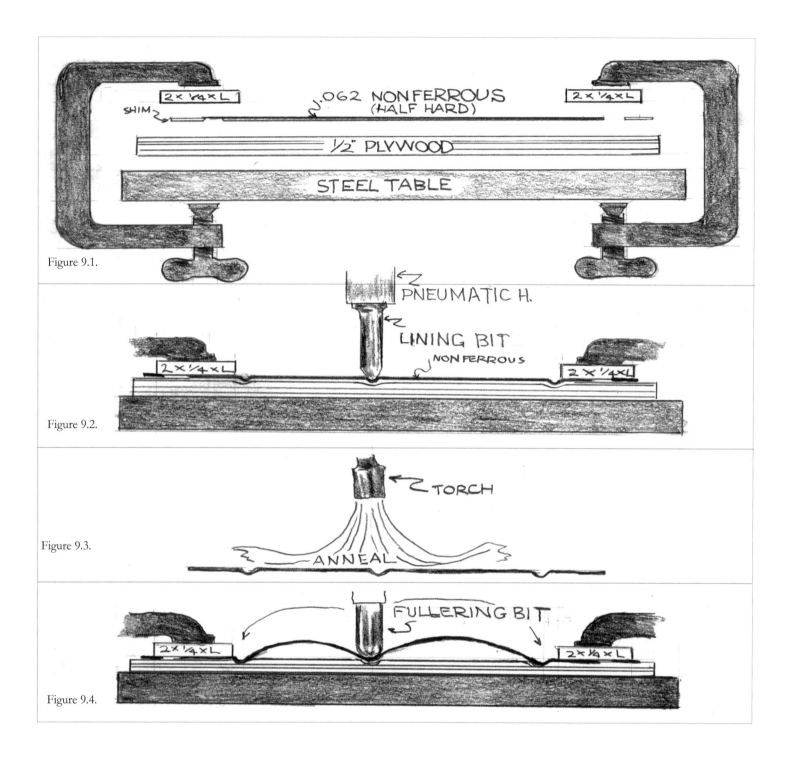

Figure 9.1.

Figure 9.2.

Figure 9.3.

Figure 9.4.

Figure 9.1. This shows how the half-hard piece of non-ferrous, which has been cut oversize, is clamped over a plywood substrate to a steel table using "C" clamps and EOP bars. The design has been sketched on the material with a felt tipped marker. Refer to Chapter 3 for a description of clamping systems.

Figure 9.2. A lining bit is used to trace the design on the half hard material.

Figure 9.3. After the material is removed from the set-up it is annealed by heating uniformly to a dull red heat followed by quenching.

Figure 9.4. The annealed work piece is reassembled over the plywood, clamped as before, and relined deeper with a broader bit, making the unlined areas bulge.

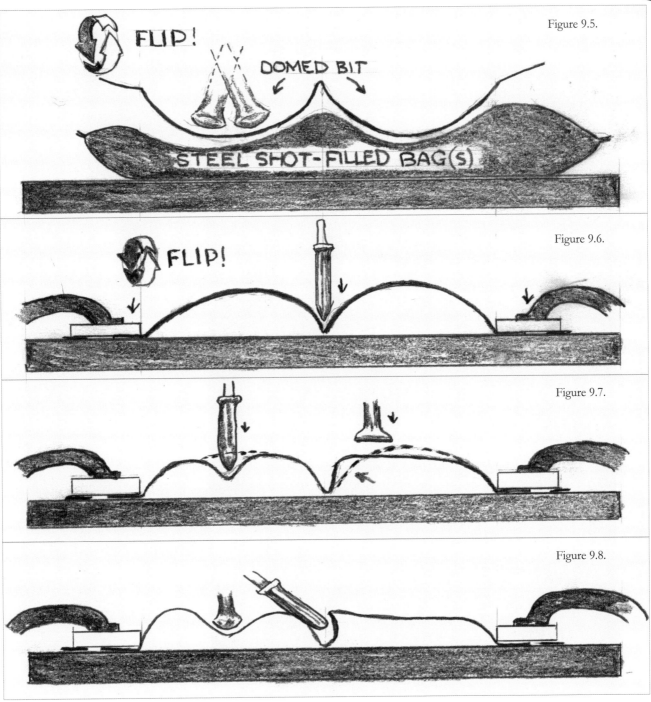

Figure 9.5.

FLIP!

DOMED BIT

STEEL SHOT-FILLED BAG(S)

Figure 9.6.

FLIP!

Figure 9.7.

Figure 9.8.

Figure 9.5. Remove from clamped position. Flip work-piece over on top of steel shot filled bag(s) and stretch the bulged areas as desired with a #15 (Chapter 2) large diameter peen.

Figure 9.6. Flip the work-piece back over. Clamp the perimeter back down to retain the base plane. Clarify the shapes as desired with the appropriate bits. If the metal is becoming work hardened anneal again. Local annealing is now possible.

Figure 9.7. Refine shapes: if some sharpened edges are desired, follow the deployment of moves shown on the right side of the work piece in this figure and in Figure 9.8.

Figure 9.8. Refinement of the forms can continue by working, flipping, and locally annealing as needed.

DEVELOPMENT OF AN ACTUAL PANEL

The following sequence of photos shows the development of an actual panel that relates to the sequence of illustrations in Figures 9.1 through 9.8.

Figure 9.9. Demonstrates the lining of the half-hard non-ferrous panel (in this case, copper) as illustrated in Figure 9.2. Note the bit used for the lining operation. Also note the use of "P" and "N" drawn on the copper; they identify what areas are to be "positive" or "negative" spaces in the design.

Figure 9.10. Annealing has been completed as in Figure 9.3 and relined as in Figure 9.4. Work has now progressed to the flip side using a shot filled leather bag as back up. Note that the "positive" "negative" identification has been retained to avoid confusion. Also the much wider bit in the hammer.

Figure 9.11. As shown in Figure 9.6, further definition of forms is proceeding with a lining bit alternating with a large diameter peen on the backside (flip). Note that whenever lining is being done it is always backed by either plywood or the shot filled bag, never directly by the steel table which would work harden the line and cause cracking.

Figure 9.12. Areas previously described as "negative" are now hammered down to the table plane to further define the "positive" forms. Note that whenever work is being done on the positive side, the piece is clamped down around the perimeter (table plane) to control distortion.

Figure 9.13. "Artistic license" prevails. Some changes have been made to, I believe, make the piece more effective. Sharpening some of the lines and adding a cutout will add to the effectiveness of the swirling dynamic. The lesson here is flexibility in rendition is part of process.

Figure 9.14. The panel is done; perimeter is trimmed and recesses are hammered in at attach points (see at bottom of this photo and Figure 9.15). Wire brushing in preparation for the acid bath that will precede patination gives the panel a glow.

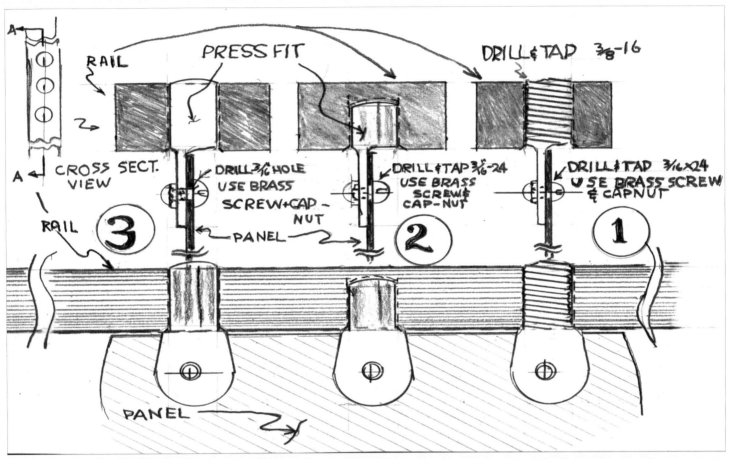

Figure 9.15. Panel retainers. Here are three versions of my preferred way of securing decorative panels of non ferrous metals to iron structures. These retainers are all forged from $3/8$ inch silicone bronze or naval brass round rod. Number 1 is threaded $3/8$-16 NC and uses a tapped hole in the iron structure. Number 2 is used in blind holes in iron structures where wetness is not a problem, and Number 3 utilizes a through hole. Panel attachments may be any of the methods shown; however, I prefer the tapped $3/16$-24 NC retainer with a cap-nut as a locking nut to discourage tampering.

RECOMMENDATION: TAKING THE LONG VIEW

Mixing metals in decorative structures presents the conundrum of how protective finishes are to be applied and maintained. Commonly, finishes for non-ferrous metals involve materials that are corrosive to steel and finishes ideal for steel do not present the best option for non-ferrous. To add to the woes, galvanic corrosion between dissimilar metals at contact areas must be considered. Integrity is at issue here: responsibility for adequate maintenance of art metalwork rests with the maker in the practical design of how these considerations are addressed. Good design should make it possible to separate the dissimilar metals for refinishing with provisions for precise relocation of the refinished work within the structure. When the original design is done with this principle in mind, restoration can be accomplished with some assurance that the integrity of the design will be maintained for the functional life of the work. Think beyond your "expiration date" and your work may survive as long as it is loved.

INCORPORATING LARGER THEME RICH NON-FERROUS IMAGES IN GATES

Part One: *The Mermaid Gate*

As stated earlier in this chapter, the addition of non-ferrous elements to steel structures requires only that they support their own mass within the design. When the inclusion is relatively large, such as the mermaid image detailed here (as opposed to panels which are supported around their periphery), a steel substructure was integral to the design. The steel frame also supported the latch mechanism which was positioned under one of the mermaid's arms. Development of the frame was coordinated to the contours by a cardboard cut-out, which was used to guide the .062 inch CDA alloy #655 silicone bronze oversize trim.

Figure 9.16. Lining one of the mermaid cutouts over plywood. Note the sketched out mermaid's hair shown in the lower right, awaiting lining. The sheet of silicone bronze will be completely lined before the first annealing.

Figure 9.17. Applying the fish scale motif to the mermaid's tail. This is done before annealing or any subsequent forming; this detailing will not be lost in the subsequent shaping of tail.

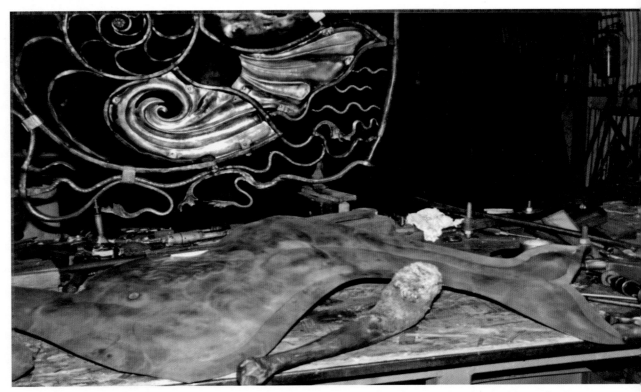

Figure 9.18. Softened by annealing, the mermaid half is rough shaped over shot filled leather bags with a large wooden mallet. The use of a soft-faced mallet retains the annealed condition of the metal, allowing considerable shaping before the use of steel pneumatic hammer bits. Note the retainer mounted panels.

Figure 9.19. More mallet work, and now starting to use the .401 hammer to further define the form, most evident in the mermaid's hair.

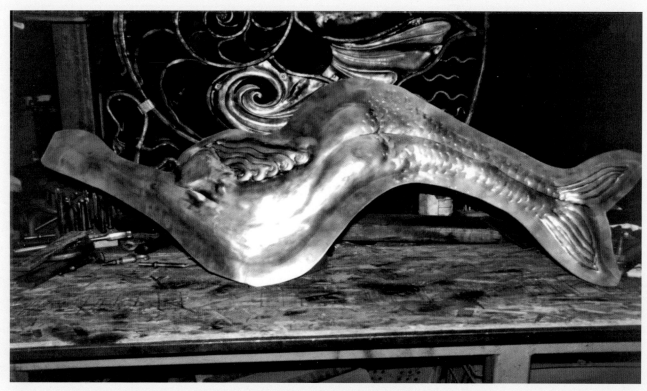

Figure 9.20. Using the .401 hammer with a large peening bit, the forms take shape. The appropriate size fullering bits are used for the tail fin and hair, alternating with lining bits to enhance definition. At this point, localized annealing is being used as needed to avoid work hardening.

Figure 9.21. Wire brushing imparts a clarifying blush to the near completed back half as the front half (sans head), finished to the same degree, swims above it. The front half, in position, is here being fitted to the iron frame that will support the figure.

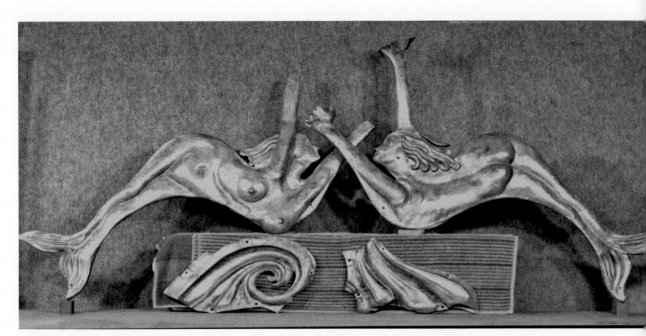

Figure 9.22. All the non-ferrous components of the Mermaid Gate are displayed just for the fun of it. Note that the front half now has its half head which had to be forged separately because of the overlapping arm.

Figure 9.23. Making the front half of the head has to be delayed until the two halves were being fitted to the frame. Note how the latch spring mechanism is designed to work under the bronze figure as part of the steel structure.

Figure 9.24. Mermaid gate. Finished and hung. Santa Cruz, California

Part Two: *"Woman With Her Head In The Clouds And A Resting Pelican"*

Figure 9.25. Gate themes can become very personal in their symbolic meaning and by doing so, touch the essence of poetry. My client for this gate was a woman who I saw as bravely facing a personal loss, who found solace in her seaside environment and particularly the seabirds. Hence, the theme.

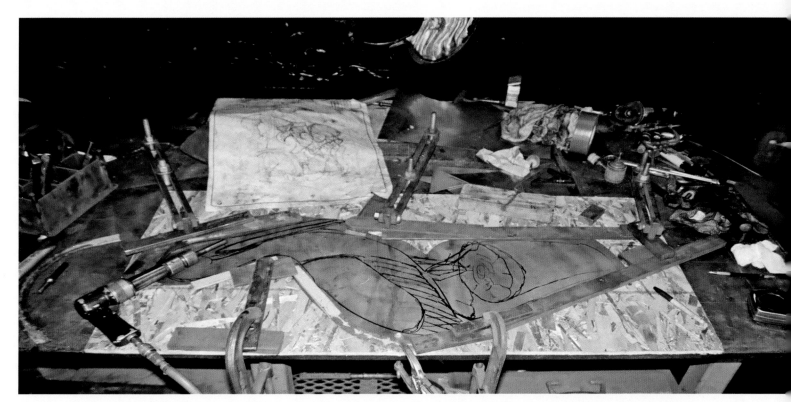

Figure 9.26. Shows the front side of the pelican cut out of half hard CDA alloy #655, .062 inch thick. Prior to this, a cardboard cut out was made from a scale drawing, followed by a $5/8$ inch diameter steel-working armature (application to be explained later). Note the felt tip pen sketch of the bird and the piling on the sheet. The piece is ready for lining to be followed by annealing.

Figure 9.27. This in-process photo of the development of the pelican's form shows how the lining, which was done in the first stage, is maintained by hammering from the back side of the sheet between the lining grooves to fill out the forms. Note the use of clamped down EOP steel bars to keep the sheet from warping.

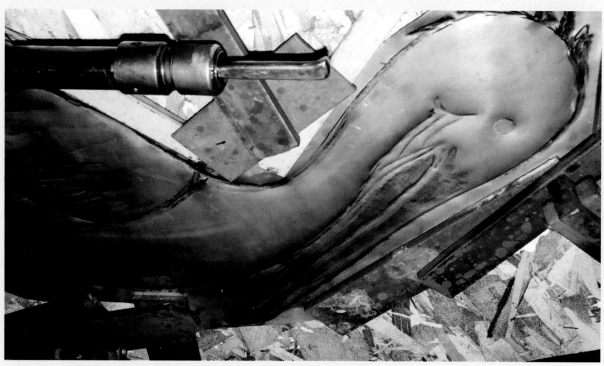

Figure 9.28. Photo showing the pelican's head and bill in work. The bit in the .401 hammer is a flatter. It was just used to work on flattening the lower part of the bill. Note how it added sharpness to the line.

Figures 9.29 and 9.30. These two (not quite matching enough to make a splice) photos show the pelican gate at the stage before the inclusion of the bird and the other panels. What it does show is the pelican's armature and the cardboard cut outs representing the panels that will be copper and stainless steel.

The pelican armature represented a new method of assembly for me; it was designed to master the profile of the two halves by using it to actually hammer-fit the edges to match, then gas welding them together. After completing the weld the bead was ground smooth and finished. The armature was then recycled.

Unfortunately, no in-process photos were taken of the other panels.

Figure 9.31. "Woman With Her Head In The Clouds And A Resting Pelican" gate. Viewed from the inside, the brass cap-nuts securing the wave themed copper panels were newly installed, clearly showing the location of the panel retainers.

Figure 9.32. "Woman With Her Head In The Clouds And A Resting Pelican" gate. Front view. Counting the stainless steel details depicting foam and the sun-ray image on the upper right, five different metals were used on this gate.

CHAPTER 10

RIVETING WITH
////////////// The //////////////
PNEUMATIC HAMMER

HAMMER (PNEUMATIC) AND ANVIL (BUCKING BAR)

Riveting uses the same physical principles as demonstrated by blacksmithing: impact constrained by inertial mass produces focused energy on what lies between the hammer and the anvil. What is unique with the handheld pneumatic hammer is that the energy is focused rapidly at many blows per minute (BPM). Riveting creates an enhanced effect when the pneumatic hammer is used in conjunction with a "bucking bar." A bucking bar, for the purposes of this definition, can mean any conveniently adapted weighty piece of steel, either handheld or somehow positioned securely to back up the rivet during "setting." Rapid blows of the hammer transfer through the rivet to the "live" response of the bucking bar. The firm pressure applied to the bucking bar by the "bucker" creates a restrained "bounciness" that translates into rapid micro-blows delivered to the rivet. This explains the rapid "setting" of the rivet on the bucking bar side and also explains where the "bucking" in "bucking bar" comes from!

There is obviously some advantage in having an assistant to "buck" during riveting, especially during so-called "blind side" operations. For reassurance, I can say that I have rarely had help with this task, yet have always found a way to get the job done. Keeping the work at the table plane is a general rule that I follow which allows me to make set-ups using stops, clamped bucking bars and even a specially adapted heavy duty forged "C" clamp (shown in Figure 10.2).

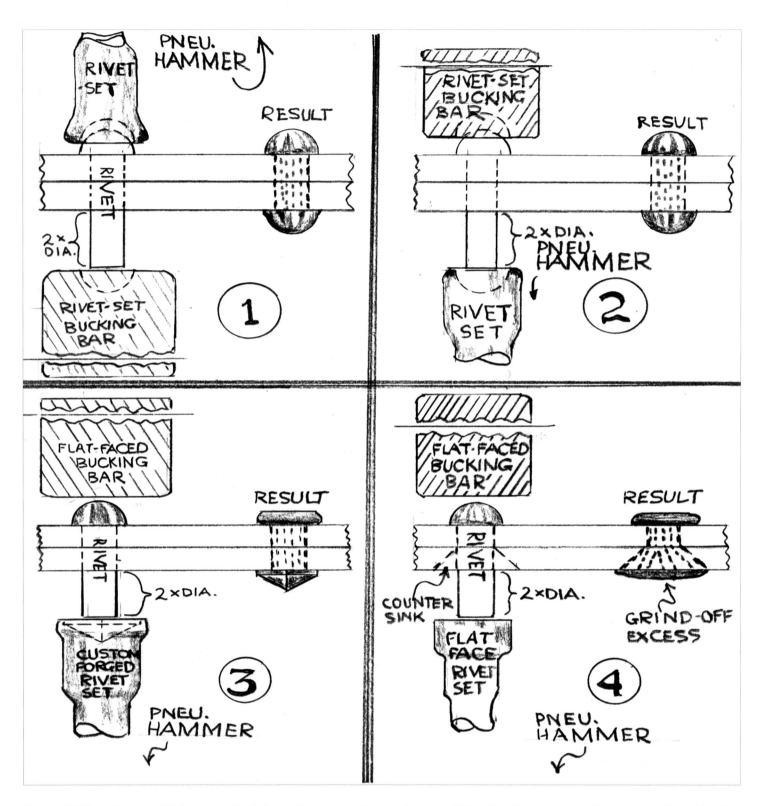

Figure 10.1. Shows four possibilities for riveting. Relationships between rivet sets (hammer side) and bucking bars can be "mix and match" combinations.

Upper left, 1, shows both rivet set and bucking bar with rivet head recess.
Upper right, 2, shows same bucking bar and rivet set with roles reversed.
Lower left, 3, shows custom forged rivet set with flat faced bucking bar.
Lower right, 4, shows both rivet set and bucking bar with flat face setting a counter sunk application with a standard rivet.

Figure 10.2. Heavy duty "C" clamp modified by welding a forged "U" section of 1 x 2 inch mild steel to serve as access to the rivet for the rivet-set equipped pneumatic hammer. Note the recess in the "C" clamp screw to accommodate the rivet head. This tool has limited applications, but can be very useful where appropriate. See Figure 10.3 below.

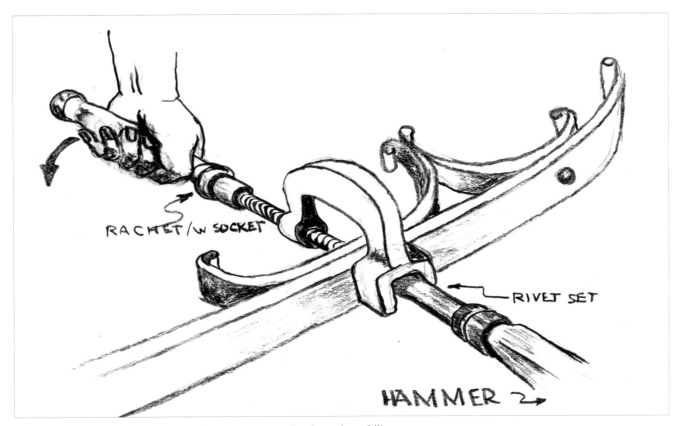

Figure 10.3. Using the modified clamp. To prevent the clamp from falling off a ratchet with socket is applied to tighten the clamp as riveting proceeds.

OTHER METHODS FOR BACKING RIVETS WHEN WORKING SOLO

Every smith who deals with the conundrum of bucking rivets without help must work out creative ways of doing it; often based on the immediate need for "never faced this dilemma before" thinking. Some "bounciness" on the bucking side is ok, even desirable, as long as a firm, controlled pressure is maintained at the hammer side of the rivet head. One very useful method of backing rivets, especially larger sizes ($3/8$ to $5/8$ inch diameter), uses a platen table equipped with a stop block, which is simply a block of hot rolled steel that fits the platen table holes and extends several inches above the surface. For riveting purposes, it may have a recess for the rivet head or not, depending on what is desired (see Figure 10.1 for choices).

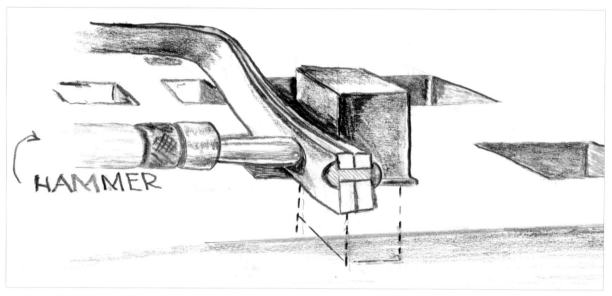

Figure 10.4. Illustrates a riveting operation in progress on a platen table using a "stop block" for bucking, and a completed rivet in cross section.

SETTING RIVETS: COLD OR HOT?

Manufacturers of pneumatic hammers designed for riveting usually supply specifications for how their tools perform on various rivet diameters (when set cold) manufactured from steel and aluminum alloy. Values for cold setting of steel rivets are given here for typical industrial .401, and .498 hammers.

Hammer, shank size	Bore	Stroke	Max. Steel Rivet Diameter, cold
0.401", type #1 (10.19mm)*	$9/16$" (14.3mm)*	4.0" (120mm)*	$3/16$"
0.498", type "D" (12.65mm)	$3/4$" (19.1mm)	7.0" (210mm)*	$3/8$" (7.9mm)

* Typical dimension for H.D. Industrial rated tool, check specifications of selected tool for comparison.

Hot setting rivets. Values for hot setting steel rivets may be hard to duplicate as one-heat operations because of the less than ideal heating of rivets during complex assembly tasks common in the artist/blacksmith shop. Rarely do I find myself with a uniformly yellow-hot rivet to quickly dispatch, in one heat, into a satisfying double headed, textbook perfect finished rivet! In most cases I use torch heat to set rivet diameters from $1/4$ inch on up through $3/8$ inch even though most specifications cover these sizes (with the proper hammer) as being okay for cold setting. For steel rivets $7/16$ to $5/8$ inch diameters it is necessary to use .680 size hammers.

"Chipping" or "Riveting"? First a little ramble about practical considerations to make in selecting a .680 size hammer for general shop use. In discussing tool selection in Chapter 1, I recommend a 4 inch stroke, $1\frac{1}{8}$ inch bore hammer as the most versatile .680 size hammer for the artist/blacksmith shop. This hammer is classified as a "chipping" hammer, not a "riveting" hammer in most catalogs. That is a distinction that can be disregarded for our purposes unless your plans include using $3/4$ inch or larger rivets that require the longer stroke, longer length, and heavier weight, found in these "riveting" tools. Enough said.

Heating rivets for hot setting. Ideally, a small rivet forge, fueled by coal or gas can be used to heat the rivet to a yellow heat; it is quickly inserted in the readied assembly and set and bucked into a perfect, finished fastener. I wish you many opportunities to fit this scenario, but often riveted assemblies in the shop require a more complex approach which may require inserting a cold rivet and setting up backup before riveting can proceed.

An oxy-fuel gas torch with a relatively small tip (determined by the size of the rivet, not the mass of the assembly) is used to heat the rivet. Bring the rivet to a yellow heat while avoiding the surrounding mass as much as possible and quickly proceed with setting. If the setting operation takes more than one heat, which it may, particularly with larger rivets, be aware that as the assembly soaks up heat from the rivet it will expand causing the rivet to set a little loose. Check rivets after the assembly has cooled and tighten any that are loose fitting by rehammering cold. Rehammered rivets must be bucked!

Tip: It is a good idea to slightly chamfer rivet holes on both sides before riveting to eliminate crack formation at these vulnerable sites.

Setting small diameter brass rivets. Brass rivets of $1/8$ to $3/16$ inch diameter such as used on kitchen hoods and other non-ferrous sheet assemblies can be readily set cold with the .401 hammer while holding a bucking bar in your opposite hand. This makes for fairly rapid assembly, especially if using a flat faced bar. Be sure to use plenty of clecos when doing rows of rivets in this manner to prevent the buckling (see Chapter 8) that would probably occur if the assembly is not tightly aligned.

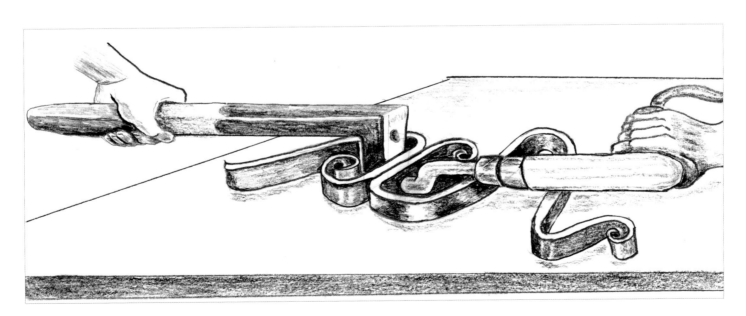

A useful riveting accessory.
Figure 10.5. Riveting in tight places may require the use of an off-set rivet header and right-angled bucking bar as pictured here.

CHAPTER 11

MATERIAL SELECTION FOR WORKING
With
PNEUMATIC HAMMERS

WROUGHT COPPER BASED ALLOYS

There are plenty of fundamental differences in the working of wrought copper based alloys to the working of mild steel. These differences have to do with conductivity, working temperature, ductility, strength, hardness, and finally, cost. The last item listed is perhaps the most significant deterrent to mastering the copper alloys. Wrought copper alloys usually cost six or more times the pound price of common low carbon steels, are heavier, and possess significantly less tensile and shear strength. These factors combined make the use of copper alloys particularly expensive for applications that require structural integrity. All are good reasons for their more selective use in larger scale metal arts. On the appealing side, these alloys are corrosion resistant in all natural environments, can be treated to display a great range of colors, and, according to the particular alloy, are very ductile either hot or cold (in some cases both).

As with conventional forging techniques, it is sensible to develop some pneumatic hammer skills on less expensive mild steel before focusing on copper alloys. That said, here are the basic working characteristics of the thicker (beyond gauge thickness) copper alloys best suited for hot forging, and of gauge thickness alloys suitable for cold forming, and in some cases, also hot working. The alloys described in this list I originally selected as the most promising for the hammer as determined by engineering material data comparisons of working properties; hands-on experience then led to my current list of favorite alloys. My subjective list is based on observations working with the particular metals. Basic characteristics such as hot or cold working preferences, ductility, work hardening, and annealing are addressed. The following list displays comparative working properties and some physical and mechanical properties that are useful to the artist smith who has limited need for engineering data. The listed technical data is taken from the Copper Development Association (CDA) specifications. I do show some very basic mechanical properties for a very rough comparison of material strength. There is a lot more to determining relative material strength according to the design application, but tensile strength and elongation (which is an indicator of ductility) are useful basics. The figures given are for annealed material, assuming that hammer work (which hardens the material) is casual and therefore does not accurately reflect hardened specifications. Forging and fabricating commentary is based on my own subjective experience working these metals.

TABLE 1: SELECTED COPPER BASED ALLOYS FOR HOT AND COLD WORKING*

CDA ALLOY #. & TYPE	NOMINAL COMPOSITION (%)	TENSILE STRENGTH annealed, (PSI)	Elongation. (2") % Annealed	WORKING TEMP. F HOT/ANNEAL/COLD			JOINING Ex=excellent Gd=good Poor=Poor
Electrolytic Pitch Copper **#110**	Cu 100	32-35,000	45-55	1400-1600 Ex.	700-1200	YES Ex.	Soldering Ex. Brazing Gd. TIG Ex.
Phosphorus Deoxidized Copper **#122**	Cu 100	32-34,000	45	1400-1600 Ex.	700-1200	YES Ex.	Soldering Ex. Brazing Ex. Welding Oxyacetylene & TIG Ex.
Jewelry Bronze **#226**	Cu 87.5 Zn 12.5	42,000	44	1400-1650 Gd.	800-1400	YES Ex.	Soldering Ex., Brazing (silver) Ex. Welding, Oxyacetylene & TIG, Gd.
Red Brass **#230**	Cu 85 Zn 15	42,000	44	1450-1650 Gd.	800-1300	YES Ex.	Soldering Ex. Brazing (Silver) Welding, Oxyacetylene& TIG, Gd.
Cartridge Brass **#260**	Cu 70 Zn 30	44-48,000	64-66	1350-1550 Fair	800-1400	YES Ex.	Soldering Ex. Brazing (silver) Welding, Oxyacetylene & TIG Gd.
Naval Brass **#464**	Cu 60 Zn 39.25 Sn 0.75	57,000	47	1400-1650 Ex.	800-1100	No Poor	Soldering Ex. Brazing (silver) Welding, Oxyacetylene & TIG Gd.
High Silicone Bronze A **#655**	Cu 94.8 Si 2.8-3.8 Mn 1.5 Zn 1.5 Fe 1.6 Ni 0.6	56-63,000	55-63	1300-1600 Ex.	900-1300	YES Ex.	Soldering Ex. Brazing (Silver) Ex. Welding Oxyacetylene Gd. TIG Ex.

*My subjective list. See the following hands-on description of working properties of the listed alloys.

CDA Alloy #110, Electrolytic Pitch Copper. Most commonly available copper, this material is available in sheet, solid bar stock, tube, and architectural shapes. It yields superbly to the hammer. It works hot very well, but be careful not to overheat (bright red), at which point the metal is crumbly and cannot be restored to working ductility; this applies to the annealing process as well. When working thicker stock, resist the temptation to maximize your heat by continuing to forge as the copper cools and work-hardening resistance appears; your piece will likely crack or split. Reserve that time for light finishing, or return the piece to your fire (coal, coke, or gas).

Cold working of annealed copper sheet or light solid stock is pleasurable with the pneumatic hammer since deformation is rapid and easily controlled. I suggest the use of a torch with a rosebud, either oxyacetylene (or any of the other torch gases) for annealing sheet stock. Once again, avoid overheating (bright red). Quenching the sheet is optional; the one advantage of quenching over ambient cooling is the temperature shock of the cool water efficiently removes most of the heat scale. Local annealing for heavily-worked areas is fine, but be sure to heat all the area to be worked and somewhat beyond. For detailed forming techniques with the pneumatic hammer see Chapter 9.

CDA Alloy #122, Phosphorus Deoxidized Copper. Working this material is essentially the same as CDA #110. This copper is used for plumbing water lines and other forms of tubing; a useful stock material.

CDA Alloy #226, Jewelry Bronze. This is a handsome material, a particularly rich raw bronze color when polished, similar to CDA #655 in color but much softer under the hammer. It is excellent working cold but requires careful attention to work hardening limits and upper temperature range cracking when worked hot. It is not usually available in plate or solid bar. This alloy can be welded with TIG and oxyacetylene and is particularly good for brazing and soft soldering.

CDA Alloy #230, Red Brass. With a zinc content just 2.5% higher than CDA #226 you correctly expect that the working properties of #230 are close. The step up in zinc means it is slightly harder at ambient temperature and is "redder" in tone. Available in sheet, strip, and unlike #226, also pipe and tube.

CDA Alloy #260, Cartridge Brass. My favorite yellow brass for cold working. The elongation for this material (annealed) is a whopping 66.65% (compare to the elongation figures for other brasses in the table). It is very good for raising deep shapes. Exercise caution, as the material work hardens (gets springy) cracking may occur. This brass should not be worked hot, even light blows will cause cracks. It welds well with TIG, but with the oxyacetylene torch, I recommend brazing or soldering. Available in almost all mill forms.

CDA Alloy #464, Naval Brass. Sometimes called Naval Bronze (I know not why. It is a yellow metal, perhaps it is because of the small percentage of tin ([0.75]). The high zinc content provides relatively high tensile strength (57 kpsi annealed and 75 kpsi half hard) approaching mild steel. This alloy is my absolute favorite brass for hot forging. This material, worked within the temperature range shown in the table, is the most plastic material I have hot worked. Do not attempt working this metal cold, it is easily fractured, even with light deformation. It is common brass brazing rod, available in diameters ranging from $1/16$ to $3/8$ inch, readily found at your welding supply dealer, a convenient source of this alloy for smaller work. Exercise care when heating sections along a bar for forging, it tends to droop like a cooked noodle. Available in most mill forms.

CDA Alloy #655, High Silicone Bronze A. My favorite copper alloy for all-round use. It forges much like mild steel. In fact, my problem hot forging this material is forgetting that it is a copper alloy instead of steel and overheating it to decomposition in the forge. One of the reasons for this misadventure is the relatively low thermal conductivity for a copper alloy. Very plastic in the hot range, it may be worked from hot to ambient temperature if you progress to light blows as it cools. Sheet material may be worked very efficiently cold if you anneal carefully first (note the elongation figures in Table 1). However, you will find that in this condition it is quite "springy" and requires heavier blows than most copper alloys for deformation. When working bar stock be sure to anneal well past the area being worked to avoid fractures. Alloy #655 is available in almost all mill forms.

Notes on copper alloys not on my "select" list. There are many other copper alloys on the market. Some I have tried such as CDA #280 Muntz Metal and #377 Forging Brass. Aluminum Bronzes #614 and #639 can also be used but in my opinion these have processing shortcomings that make them less desirable. Many of the other alloys have some lead content for machining lubricity which I feel should be avoided. Others are for specialized applications and not usually available in the mill forms usable by the smith.

Empirical use of engineering data on material properties. As you read in the previous section, I gave some examples of the relationship of engineering data to material selection. It is very useful to be able to reference mechanical and physical properties as part of your material selection process. Many specifications can be empirically used by the artist by comparing hands-on working observations with numerical specifications data.

As an example, here are the comparative mechanical properties for mild steel and copper alloy #110. Mild steel: tensile strength, 60-70 kpsi; elongation (in two inches), 20%-30%. Copper UNS (United Numbering System), CDA #110: tensile strength, 32-35 kpsi; elongation (in two inches), 45%-55%. Alloy #110 is the most commonly available copper used in architectural applications. Other unalloyed coppers are similar.

A comparison of the tensile strength figures representing these two metals shows the mild steel to be twice as strong in tension as the copper. This is an important consideration if your project, to some extent almost all free standing work, must have structural integrity. Elongation figures reflect the higher ductility of the copper, telling us what our hands know from working the metal. Use technical data to gather some sense of a metal's profile. If you compare this abstract data to the empirical hands on work, some feeling for what the data really is profiling emerges. By comparing physical and mechanical test data of metals, and filtering these relative properties with the screen of subjective hands on experience with similar metals, it becomes possible to "read" some engineering properties well enough for them to be useful aides in material selection.

Other non-ferrous metals applicable to pneumatic hammer forging such as aluminum, tin, and zinc alloys have not been included by the author simply because I dislike the "feel" of these metals under the hammer.

But aluminum is a very versatile metal, its light weight can be used to advantage in structural applications. The "purer" alloys, such as #1100, also have good corrosion resistance and very high initial ductility but tend to work harden rapidly; annealing (650 F.) should be frequent. Some of the high strength alloys can be heat treated up to mechanical levels approaching low carbon steel. As an example #6061, heat treated to T-6 has a tensile strength of 45,000 psi compared to 73,000 psi for c1050 steel. Aluminum can also be protected by "anodizing," a process that "converts" the surface of the aluminum to an inorganic layer of very high corrosion resistance. A wide range of colors are possible with this process. On the negative side, aluminum tends to "gaul" during forming, the metal tends to adhere to the tools and not form cleanly. If this metal intrigues you, by all means try it!

CHAPTER 12

FURNISHING A WORKSPACE
With
PNEUMATIC TOOLS

Is it for you? This may not be everyone's solution to portable power tools in their workspace. Your shop's compressor would be running much of the time pneumatic tools are being used, and the tools themselves will join in the chorus to create quite a din, shattering your peace of mind. Well, you can mitigate some of the racket by locating the compressor out of earshot and conscientiously wearing ear protection, and, like me, learning to love the screeches, howls, and whines the tools create as they efficiently do their jobs. The operative word here is "efficiently". As I have said throughout this book, from my personal experience, quality pneumatic tools are lighter, more powerful, and more durable than their electric counterparts; all you must do is keep them lubricated!

Unlike my recommendations for pneumatic hammers, which are biased toward "industrial" grade tools, I feel it is adequate to go with "automotive" grade tools of good quality for most other applications if your choices meet your performance standards. The reason for this concession is cost. "Industrial" quality hammers will give you the high tactile performance you will need to satisfy your artistic needs, but mechanical operations such as drilling and grinding can be satisfied on a more pragmatic "automotive" level. This is my rationalization to keep control of my tool budget since you may realize a 35% to 40% savings by accepting a reasonable sacrifice in performance where it probably would be hard to measure.

The selection of tool types covered in this chapter is limited to those I have personally used. These are carefully chosen tools, many of them have been doing their job for years, covering the basic functions appropriate to our craft. There are many other types of tools that perform more specialized functions available from your local pneumatic tool supplier. Enjoy the variety if you are a "tool nut," but for simplicity, this group of tools should serve you well.

PORTABLE DRILLS

These tools are identified by the chuck size, which, in turn, is determined by the drilling capacity of the tool, a function of air consumption and RPM. In general, the smaller capacity drills have higher RPM which matches the general rule that smaller drills may be operated at higher RPM and require less torque than larger drills.

Like all air tools, and unlike electric drills, air drills are not damaged by stalling or jamming, simply back the tool off the jam and resume work. With all drills RPMs are specified for greatest utility.

¼ inch drills. A relatively high speed drill, often achieving 2500 to 3000 RPM. These tools are small and light, useful for light drilling, reaming, and abrasive applications with drum sanders, PSA (pressure sensitive adhesive) disc sanding and other lightweight abrading tasks; available in (recommended) reversible models.

⅜ inch drills. A heavier tool than the ¼ inch, they are designed to operate generally in the 1500 to 2200 RPM range and consume more air because of the higher torque requirements of drilling holes of up to ⅜ inch in steel. They are not ideally used with abrasive tooling for surface finishing when higher speed (and lighter) tools are available.

Tip: The ⅜ inch drill can be used with a keyless chuck for quick changing of drill sizes often necessary in this range of drilling, available in reversible models and highly recommended for backing off seized drills.

½ inch drills. This drill is a performance marvel for its size compared to a bulky, electric drill of the same capacity. They are available in several RPM ratings under 1000. My preference is a 400 RPM model which is triple reduction geared and equipped with a side handle.

HIGH SPEED GRINDERS

For removing metal, pneumatic grinders are compact, light weight, powerful, and consume relatively lots of compressed air because the impeller that drives the tool must be equal to the free speed of the tool.

¼ inch die grinder. One of the handiest tools in the metal shop, it usually operates at 20,000 to 25,000 RPM (free speed). They work really well with carbide burrs for fast and controllable metal removal. Mounted abrasive stones are also available in many shapes and grits. These grinders are made in 90° and in-line configurations; I suggest having both for maximum utility.

Caution: Carbide burrs produce needle-sharp waste; eye protection and leather gloves are particularly important! And respiratory protection should be worn during any powered metal reducing or finishing process.

4 inch diameter disc grinder. This tool is much more compact than its electric counterpart and produces 12,000 RPM with great torque. I find it comfortable for one hand use. But the design does provide a second handle for two-handed use and I recommend its use. It is very efficient for operations using depressed grinding wheels and cutoff wheels, all configurations of wire wheels, and may even be used with a ¼ inch chuck for almost unlimited shank mounted abrasive and finishing tasks. Stalling this tool from excessive pressure or jamming will not damage it; simply back off and resume work.

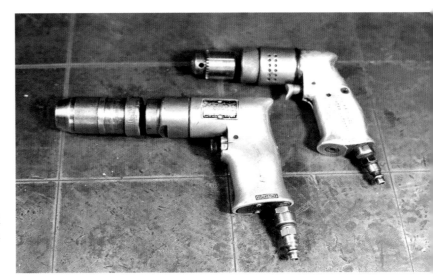

Figure 12.1 Showing the $^{1}/4$ inch drill and the $^{3}/8$ inch drill together for size comparison. Note the quick release chuck on the $^{3}/8$ inch drill.

Figure 12.2. The $^{1}/2$ inch drill shown here was shop modified to make the side handle more substantial. The heavy duty Jacobs ball bearing chuck shown is also an add-on. Modifications to original equipment is sometimes necessary to maximize performance. Try to avoid the inferior chucks usually sold with drills. That is definitely essential; the drill has enough torque to pull the tool out of the hands of an inattentive operator if it binds. Using step-drilling techniques, I have drilled many $^{3}/4$ inch holes in one inch steel plate with this tool by stepping up from $^{1}/2$ inch to $^{3}/4$ inch in $^{1}/8$ inch increments. I prefer using a keyed, heavy duty ball bearing chuck on $^{1}/2$ inch drills. The reversible model is definitely essential.

Figure 12.3. Two high speed grinders shown here will handle all $^{1}/4$ inch shank carbide burrs, and mounted grinding and polishing tasks. I recommend both the in-line and 90° designs.

Figure 12.4. 4 inch diameter disc grinder, here shown with a removable cup wire wheel for heavy duty cleaning. This grinder comes with a side handle (note the threaded hole) for two hand operation which is recommended for all applications.

7 and 9 inch disc grinders and large cone grinders. Large, heavy duty air powered grinders present a dilemma for the smaller shops equipped with a modest sized compressor. They require a lot of air, commonly 30 to 40 cubic feet per minute at 90 psi. This demand requires a very large compressor and holding tank, usually out of reach for the smaller shops. The advantage for the big industrial facilities is the savings in equipment repair and labor-friendly weight and safety features. For example, a pneumatic 9 inch grinder will weigh in at less than 10 pounds compared to approximately 27 pounds for an electric grinder of comparable performance!

I use an electric 9 inch grinder, reluctantly and not very often; it is the only electric portable tool in my shop.

There are, of course, many other pneumatic tools that could be added to this list that would be useful if found at the "right" price. Be aware of used and surplus pneumatic tool markets as found on eBay and other online sources. If you have access to surplus sales at aircraft or automotive factories, great buys can be found if you shop carefully to separate useful tools from junk. Familiarity with manufacturers and model numbers can be handy. You will find that the most desirable tools are hotly pursued by informed buyers. Remember my "Serendipitous Tale" in the Introduction?

GALLERY OF SELECTED WORKS REPRESENTATIVE
//////////////////////////// Of The Use Of The //////////////////////////////
HANDHELD PNEUMATIC HAMMER

The first section of this "gallery" shows seven photographs of finished works created using only the handheld pneumatic hammer.

Pierced Folding Sheet Wall Piece, 1980
Copper, bronze and stainless steel
60" high, 49" wide

Chimney Gargoyle, 1993
Forged copper
36" high, 42" wide

"A Child's Fantasy" wall piece, 1984
Forged .062 copper and brass
84" wide, 64" high

Note the .401 pneumatic hammer used to forge this piece in the lower left corner of the photo.

Detail of *"A Child's Fantasy"*
wall piece

"Shore Birds" fireplace surround, 1990
Forged 062 copper, brass, and bronze

Detail *"Shore Birds"*
fireplace surround

Ocean motif kitchen hood, 1998
Forged .062 copper and bronze
42" wide, 50" high

This section of the gallery is proportionally longer than the pneumatic hammer section as my work here reflects the full spectrum of metalsmithing techniques. What I have chosen to display is work where the handheld pneumatic hammer's role is significant to the finished piece.

Breeze, 1974
Forged steel and copper
20" high

Cape and all figure detailing done with pneumatic hammer.

Napping Cat with Squirrel and Bird, 1997
Steel, copper and bronze

The anxious squirrel and nesting bird panels and incised bark all pneumatic hammer wrought. The cat, if awake and aware of the little drama he was creating, could enjoy and un-cat like chuckle.

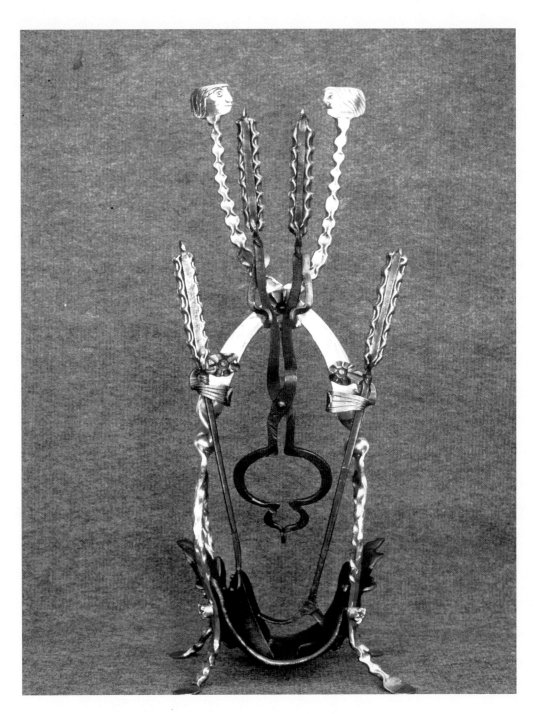

Wedding gift fireplace tool set and stand, 2004
Forged chromemoly steel, stainless steel and bronze

All steel detailing, tool handle forging, stainless steel
and bronze details are done with pneumatic hammer.

Horse Heads fireplace tool set, 1986
Chrome-moly steel and brass

All brass and steel detailing is pneumatic hammer.

Mayan motif chandelier, 1996
Steel and copper (two units)
52" long, 37" wide

All incising on steel and all work on copper
were done with pneumatic hammer.

Hanging Gargoyle, 2004
Steel and copper
17" long, 27" high

Detail of completed sculpture with progress graphics in chapter 5. All detailing with pneumatic hammer.

Wisteria Lamp, 1995
Forged steel, bronze, brass and copper
84" high

The incised bark on the copper trunk, detailing of copper
base and brass detailing work done with pneumatic hammer.

Yellow Roses with Preening Swans, 1995
Forged steel, bronze and brass
82" high

All detailing on the lamp including swans, flowers and base done with pneumatic hammer.

Yellow Roses with Preening Swans, detail

Celebrating Gaia, detail, 1990
Forged iron and stainless steel

"OH!", 1991
Forged steel
12" high

All detailing by pneumatic hammer.

Where the Ancients Got It Wrong, 2006
 Forged steel, bronze, brass and stainless steel
7' long

Pampas Grass stair railing, 1983
Forged steel, brass and bronze

All detailing by pneumatic hammer.

Plumed Horse Gate, 1984
70" high, 48" wide

Steel detailing, bronze plumes and copper panels by pneumatic hammer.

Cougar Gate opening station, 1989, cougar motif
Forged $1/4$ inch thick plate steel

The Cougar Gate, 1986
The all forged gate weighs two tons

This gate was designed to capture what Los Gatos once meant;
it translates to "the cats" in Spanish, so named because the hilly,
live oak forest and grassland country once supported a healthy
cougar population. The cougars are gone from loss of habitat;
the image now exists in iron.

ABOUT
~~~~~~ The ~~~~~~
AUTHOR

What are the ingredients in building a career? I suppose the logical answer would be something like this: decide what you want to do and concentrate on fulfilling all the requirements needed to achieve that goal. Well, what if what you want to achieve is too nebulous to be defined handily, no less specifically, as "goal"; maybe it is more like an indistinct yearning somewhere in your imagined life that is motivating your actions. What if you decide to call this curious pursuit "ART"? Now you've done it; swooning over a muse who doesn't clearly define the world in easily structured segments, but instead leads you down a random path allowing blurry glimpses of the "larger picture," not to look at, but hopefully, to see.

And, what if along with this indistinct yearning you have a very tangible inclination to work physically in three dimensions while thinking abstractly? If you are a smith, you have a better idea of where my inclinations were driving me than my youthful self understood.

Along the way I studied figure drawing at the Art Students League while attending New York's High School of Music and Art. Then heading downtown to Cooper Union Institute, I majored in Fine Arts with a minor in Architecture.

On my trail to self sufficiency I worked at many things that seem remote to someone supposedly pursuing a career in art: advertising, display builder, woodcarver, plaster mock-up, plastic tooling, lofting, planning, engineering consultant, and materials research engineer, and, all through this seemingly unconnected pastiche, working on and exhibiting sculpture. Ironically, the sculpture often reflected the materials and techniques I had become familiar with in my industrial and technological working life. It all came together as I finally found my focus in metalsmithing by then it was the mid 1960's and my "so called career" was now on track. Amazingly, all the pieces of my puzzle fit to make a unified whole, resulting in my art and craft.

As you access this book, I think you will see how the sum of experience creates a total of one person.

Over the past forty years all of my creative energy has been focused on metalsmithing. During this time, I have had two National Endowment for the Arts grants, participated in metal art exhibitions in Canada, the U.K., many locations in the U. S., demonstrated and lectured at many conferences sponsored by the Artist-Blacksmith's Association of North America (ABANA), the California Blacksmith Association (CBA), and the Northwest Blacksmith Association (NWBA), written numerous essays and articles on art and metalwork for many publications, and taught at Penland School Crafts in North Carolina. In 2006, just three years before I retired from my forge I received the coveted career achievement award from ABANA, called the Alex Bealer Award. I finally had the time to finish this book.

INDEX

Italics and letter f indicate photograph or figure.

A
A Child's Fantasy, f124
air compresssor, 23
air tools. *See* pneumatic tools.
anvil, 107–109

B
backboard, kitchen hood, 88
ball type safety retainer, 4
basic hammer control, 33–35, *f34*
"beehive" retainer, 4
blocking out, 44
blows per minute (BPM), 1
botanical themes. *See* floral designs
brands of hammers, 2
Breeze, f127
bucking bar, 107–109, *f108–109*

C
"C" clamps, 30
candlestick, *f67*
Celebrating Gaia, f135
chameleon, *f47*
Chimney Gargoyle, f123
chisel blanks, 7
clamping "hold downs", 25, *f25–26*
clamping systems, 27–28, *f27–28*
Clecos, *f80*
cold marking, 35
cold marking process, 36–38, *f36–37*
contour control, *f74–76*
copper based alloys
    CDA Alloy #110, Electrolytic Pitch Copper, 115
    CDA Alloy #122, Phosphorus Deoxidized Copper, 115
    CDA Alloy #226 Jewelry Bronze, 115
    CDA Alloy #230, Red Brass, 115
    CDA Alloy, #260 Cartridge Brass, 115
    CDA Alloy, #464, Naval Brass, 115
    CDA Alloy, #655, 115
    information on, 113–114
    notes on, 116
    use of engineering data on material properties, 116
Copper Development Association (CDA), 113
copycat hammers, 1
corner and radius tool bits
    32, 20, *f20*

The Cougar Gate, 54–57
The Cougar Gate, f54–57, 141
Cougar Gate opening Station, 140
couplers and hoses, 5
cubic feet per minute (CFM), 23
cutting, incising and lining tool bits. *See* tool bits

D
descaling and cleaning, 48
design, tool bits
    .680 tool bits, 11
    information on, 11, *f12–13*
drag technique, 33, *f34*

E
eBay, as tool market, 2
end of parts (EOP), 30
embossing tool bits. *See* tool bits
eye tool bits. *See* tool bits

F
"F" shape slide adjusting clamps, 30
fauna, features of, 47–48, *f47–48*
ferret, *f48*
finishing and tempering tool bits
    final polishing, 14–15
    rough finishing, 14–15
flanges, 82
flatter/planishing tool bits. *See* tool bits
floral designs
    assembled, *f62–64*
    creating, 59–61, *f59–61*
    leaves, grasses and other forms, 65–68, *f65–68*
    tapered stems, 69–71, *f69–71*
    wisteria and magnolia blossoms (non-ferrous), 62–64, *f62–64*
flux chipper/scaler, *f4*
forging
    plate steel, 54–57, *f54–57*
    sheet steel, 49–53, *f49–53*
forging, tool bits
    .401 and .498 tool bits, 13
    .680 tool bits, 14
    tapered and simple ended bits, 13–14
Full Moon at High Tide, f53
fullering tool bits. *See* tool bits